D0340356

The
Landau
Strategy

The Landau Strategy

HOW WORKING WOMEN
WIN TOP JOBS

Suzanne Landau and Geoffrey Bailey

Clarkson N. Potter, Inc./Publishers NEW YORK
DISTRIBUTED BY CROWN PUBLISHERS, INC.

Library of Congress Cataloging in Publication Data

Landau, Suzanne.
  The Landau strategy.

  1. Vocation guidance for women.   2. Résumés (Employment)   3. Employment interviewing.
I. Bailey, Geoffrey, 1946–   joint author.   II. Title.
HF5381.L289   1980   650′.14′02042   79-23874
ISBN: 0-517-540452

Printed in the United States of America
Published simultaneously in Canada by Lester & Orpen Dennys Limited

Designed by Robert Bull.

For Gwen & John, Cela & Izy

CONTENTS

ACKNOWLEDGMENTS

Innumerable people helped us while we researched and wrote this book. They include J. P. Allemand, Gerry De Rose, Eveleen Dollery, Barbara Faigin, Judy Farquharson, Morwena Given, Corinna Golden, Alan Gregory, Patti Gornish, Eileen Harris, Ann Hoshimi, Claire McDaniel, Marilyn March, John Quirk, June Robinson, Jeannine Rousseau, Kathy Sampson, Margaret Sharkey, Sid Simon, Linda Sobel, Mary Tapissier, Carol Tavris, John Winckler.

The opinions, criticisms, and insights of several others were crucial to the book's intellectual direction and final content. They include Elayne Bernay, Walter Bohatsch, Sheila Dillon, Carolyn Friedman, Carole Gabay, Elizabeth Hall, Peter Koenig, Carol Loblaw, Ian Macgregor, Ellen Sills-Levy, John Stratton, Marina Sturdza, Laurie Weber, Shelley Wilensky.

Two people, however, were uniquely and intimately involved in the development of *The Landau Strategy* right from the start. They are our agent, Nancy Colbert, and our editor, Barbara Purchase.

We thank them all.

INTRODUCTION

The Landau Strategy: How Working Women Win Top Jobs
deals with the long-term strategic planning and the
short-term execution of a job hunt. It is a tough-minded,
rigorous manual designed to show how the shrewd application of a few modern marketing techniques, in combination with some proven bargaining maneuvers, can enable
women to secure the kinds of jobs to which their talent
entitles them.

The book is built around three simple propositions.
First, that women have to work significantly harder than
men to secure those really first-rate jobs: for talented men,
getting a good job is just another deal to be done; for
talented women, getting a comparable job can be a major
psychological and intellectual effort.

Second, that in order to even up the male/female competitive odds, female job hunters need to adopt a special
kind of tactical planning, one that makes substantial use
of several key techniques of modern marketing.

Third, that however aggressive and persistent women
are, they tend to lack experience and know-how in the
craft of business negotiation. When it comes to the financial details of a job offer, they all too often sell themselves
short. *The Landau Strategy* contains a comprehensive dis-

cussion, supported by several specific examples, of the maneuverings necessary to close job opportunities once they have been developed.

Some readers may find a number of the views and recommendations presented in this book rather brutal and self-regarding. This is entirely intentional. Women, especially ambitious urban women, live in a highly competitive working environment where the supreme prizes go to those who are fast, strong, imaginative, and have the courage to dare; an environment from which the weak and less resourceful are mercilessly squeezed out.

Women, in our view, must learn to seize opportunities for self-advancement in the same way so many successful men do: coolly, purposefully, directly. Men have been reared to recognize that top jobs are expropriated, won. We believe that it's about time women did, too. Feminine self-effacement, that standard item of quasi-moral, quasi-social camouflage behind which so many talented women have preferred to hide for so long is, we like to think, firmly on its way out. The only value it has now, certainly the only value it has in business life, is when it is deliberately and shrewdly used as a technique of persuasion.

For women, winning that top job is a reflective, considered, therapeutic process. Psychologically, it's asking yourself exactly what you want to become. Intellectually, it's analyzing your employment objectives and identifying your best and most logical means of achieving them. Promotionally, it involves a brief but satisfying high dive into the frenetic world of hype.

The underlying argument of *The Landau Strategy* is ultimately reducible to this: the modern job hunt is best conceived not as a pleasant excursion into the niceties of public relations, but rather as a disciplined crusade into the world of marketing.

Marketing, a generic term that suggests the entire process by which a product is developed, distributed, and sold, has a wide and varied application to the special problems women confront in the job hunt. The key to the solution of those special problems is contained in the word *product*.

A woman on the job market is, her entirely reasonable feminist instincts notwithstanding, not a person but a product. The success of your job hunt will turn, in our belief, upon your ability to analyze yourself as a product in precisely the same way a marketing executive analyzes a brand: as something whose successful sale to the consumer is intimately connected to the way it is packaged, the care with which it is positioned against its potential buyers, and the manner in which it is promoted. The professionally executed marketing effort has as its objective multiple product sales; the top-job hunt has as its objective multiple job offers. The only difference between the two is that you will negotiate the job offer that meets your working and salary requirements, and reject the rest.

The Landau Strategy is divided into three sections. The first, called "Planning," deals with the problems associated with the initial details and administrative bureaucracy of a job hunt. "Planning" is about how the female job hunter should define and reach her target market, identify her objectives, research source material, and set up some basic mailing systems. Further, "Planning" identifies the female job hunter's enemies—the people and the pressures that can cause her to fail—and analyzes the underlying logic of the job hunt so that she can maximize her chances of eventual success.

Part Two is called "Promotion." Concerned fundamentally with the art of self-advertisement, "Promotion" applies the linguistic and design techniques of modern marketing to the female job hunt. "Promotion" presents original, fresh alternatives to the tired, overworked clichés of résumé and letter writing. This section shows you how to merchandise yourself successfully to the widest possible range of employment prospects; it suggests the ways in which the structure of corporate hierarchies affects final hiring decisions.

Part Three, "Making Your Sale," deals with selling psychology, selling strategy, and the tactics of job negotiation. The centerpiece of the entire book is contained in this section. It is the chapter entitled "The Interview." The interview (or rather interviews, since we expect that anyone who follows the precepts laid down in this book will be invited to attend an enormous number) is the female job hunter's main chance. It is the *management* of that main chance that so few books on the job hunt cover effectively. We do. We analyze, on a case-by-case basis, the kind of selling style to use in the interview situation, and the precise context in which to use it. We tell you about the hard sell, the soft sell, the oversell and the undersell. We talk about hard selling with a soft-sell style—women's special and most effective resource. More importantly, we deal in detail with the techniques of closing job opportunities once they've been developed: how to negotiate salaries, fringe benefits, how to prenegotiate raises; how to ensure, in short, that you win your best possible financial deal.

Throughout the text of *The Landau Strategy* there are analytical profiles of enterprising, successful women, many of whom have an instinctive understanding of the strategies we discuss. But there are also profiles of no less formidable women who, only too well aware of the mistakes they made on the way up, seem to have gained prominent job positions almost by default. We think you can learn a great deal from their errors.

Unlike most job-hunting guides, we have made a number of assumptions about the intelligence, literacy, humor, worldliness, skepticism, and plain good sense of those for whom this book is written. We assume, for instance, that you know how to write a letter. All we do is show you how to write one that snaps, crackles, and pops. You know how to use the telephone. We explain how to do so to your advantage. You know how to dress for a business meeting. We tell you how to dress shrewdly.

One thing you should never lose sight of during your campaign is just how cold-blooded an undertaking getting a job can be. Remember, a job is a contractual arrangement through which you will be asked to work in return for an agreed fee. There are few favors offered in a job negotiation. The person with the authority to hire you knows that. You should too.

Getting a job is striking a bargain. The harder you bargain, the better your chances will be of winning the job you want.

PART ONE
PLANNING

1

PREPARATION

THE DRIVING LOGIC behind professional marketing operations is the logic of preparation. That same logic should be behind your job hunt. Without preparation, your moves will lack focus, cohesion. The more complete your preparation, the more effective your eventual selling effort will be. An exhaustively prepared sale is a confident sale. You'll come across stronger, freer. Confident people get hired.

Preparation is smart tactically, too. Consider this: if an ad appears in a newspaper indicating an opening somewhere, a properly prepared job hunter can literally pick up two items of preprinted paper, type an envelope, affix a stamp, mail the complete package, and wait for a response.

But being physically prepared is not enough; you need to be psychologically prepared as well. Make no mistake about it—a full-scale job-hunting campaign can be hard going: hard on your administrative capabilities and particularly hard on your nerves. Not only must you cope with the potential organizational drudgery that can burden anyone, man or woman, when planning a job hunt, you must also face up to the grim possibility that even if you really hustle, chances are that a *man* will win the job you're after and be offered more money for it.

Study after study shows that despite the many advances working women have made, both in terms of pay and professional status, they still lag seriously behind men. The *New York Times* (January 6, 1975), reporting on "Women, Men and the Doctorate," a research program organized by the Educational Testing Service, Princeton, revealed that the average income of women five years after obtaining a Ph.D. was $16,400, while that of men was $18,700. And the gap widened with the passage of time, the average income of women twenty-two years after obtaining a Ph.D. being $21,000, while that of men was $27,000. Not a large percentage of the population (men or women) have their doctorates, yet even at this supposedly enlightened level, unfair biases obviously exist.

A more recent study, conducted by the Dartnell Institute of Business Research, Chicago, in 1979, disclosed that despite the Equal Pay Act of 1963 (amended in 1972), which requires every employer to pay equal salaries and wages without regard to sex, men in entry-level management positions can expect to receive an average salary of $16,564—4 percent more than women, who begin at $15,907.

Some authorities express the wage difference in even

more extreme terms: "On a national average, women are paid half men's salaries. In specific categories such as college graduates, or professional and technical specialty jobs, women get two-thirds of what men get in their paychecks" (Betty Lehan Harragan, *Games Mother Never Taught You*).

Our own investigations produced equally distressing results. We found that an employer's propensity to hire men (and to pay them more into the bargain) is quite as marked as Harragan suggests. All of which goes to confirm that women have an especially rugged fight on their hands in winning a top job. Our advice is simple and to the point: recognize that men have an early, inequitable job-hunting lead, and cut into that lead with superb planning.

And that starts now.

Move crisply into your campaign preparations. Here is a six-stage checklist of moves (only number 3 is especially time-consuming) that will help you pick up that vital early planning rhythm. The job hunt, like squash, is a game of momentum. Try to hit a fluent, aggressive opening stride.

1. State your objectives
2. Define your target market
3. Maintain your campaign files
4. Establish your mailing systems
5. Create your PR stance
6. Analyze your costs

1. State Your Objectives

Sounds obvious? Perhaps. But precious few people involved in job hunting ever do it. Most overlook it completely and, as a consequence, initiate their campaign on an incoherent, defensive note. Find answers to the following kinds of questions.

- In what field do I want to work?
- Where, in terms of geographical location, do I want to work?
- In what kind of organization would I prefer to be employed: a major corporation? a mid-size company? a small firm?
- How much do I want to earn: initially, and after two or three years?

Nothing impresses a potential employer more than a candidate whose career objectives are detailed, clear, and firmly held. *Women need to be especially well prepared in this area, for they are commonly supposed to be vaguer about their ambitions than men.*

Case Study: Robyn Richardson, Market Research

Robyn Richardson is a young Boston woman who won a highly paid job in New York. Before putting herself on the job market she, with the ruthless detachment of a product manager establishing the market potential for a brand, analyzed precisely what her exact employment objectives were.

"Sure," she said, "I thought through my goals very carefully. The simple process of doing that showed I had more than one—I had three!"

Robyn Richardson's objectives were easy to formulate; here's a summary of her thinking.

With a background in industrial market research (she had worked for a manufacturer of electrical carbon products) and a three-year spell as an analyst with a market research agency in Boston (working in three research areas: beverage alcohol, automobiles, cosmetics), Robyn Richardson felt that her career would benefit from a period working in New York, preferably with the research department of an advertising agency. Her objectives, therefore, were as follows:

Primary Objective: to secure employment as a research analyst in the research department of a New York advertising agency. Salary range: $20,000–$25,000

Secondary Objective: to secure employment as a research analyst in the research department of a New York company operating in an appropriate field, i.e., beverage alcohol, automobiles, cosmetics

Tertiary Objective: to secure employment with a New York market research agency

Robyn Richardson justified this trio of objectives by saying that she wanted to cover the possibility that a direct move from a Boston market research agency to a New York advertising agency might be difficult. Consequently, she was prepared to adopt a stepping-stone strategy, one that allowed her to work in a company or in another market research agency as a brief prelude to a full advertising agency assignment.

The establishment of your objectives can be as complex or as straightforward as your employment background and career ambitions dictate. Another woman with whom we spoke, employed as the financial manager of a small marine insurance company in Los Angeles, and who agreed that a statement of one's objectives was crucial in the planning stages of a job hunt, said: "My objectives for my last move were simple. I had financial experience, marine insurance experience, and some, not much, management experience. So I shuffled the pack and started selling myself as a potential financial manager in a marine insurance company. Simple."

A job hunter's objectives are the intellectual foundations upon which every move in a job-hunting campaign is built. Your objectives determine your job-hunting style and strategy. Get your objectives right the first time. Once established, the next logical step is to consider where those objectives point in terms of a target market. In some instances, you will find that the definition of your target market simply amounts to a more precise restatement of your objectives.

2. Define Your Target Market

In the case of Robyn Richardson, her target market might have been defined by the following five categories:

- Advertising agency research departments
- Company research departments, beverage alcohol
- Company research departments, automobiles
- Company research departments, cosmetics
- Market research companies

Beyond that, Robyn Richardson then identified those individuals within each category who had the authority to hire her. The logistics of this step necessarily vary from individual to individual, depending on knowledge of the industry, personal contacts, and so forth. However, should you be at a loss as to how to go about securing the names and positions of your prospects, most central libraries contain business directories, catalogued on an industry-by-industry basis, in which the names and job titles of senior personnel in various businesses can be found. Failing that, the professional association operating in the area that interests you (the listing for which you can locate in the Yellow Pages) will be only too happy to provide you with suitable names, titles, and addresses from their own compiled lists.

For most female job hunters, a multi-target market definition may not be necessary. One woman we interviewed, who works as an executive with a brokerage concern dealing in industrial and agricultural chemicals and who, before that, had been a high school teacher in general science, defined the target market for her job hunt in a far looser way.

All she really wanted to do was escape from what she referred to as "the deadening, poorly paid grind" of teaching children, into something more exciting and lucrative. It so happened that her educational background was strong in scientific subjects, particularly chemistry, a consideration which led her to believe it was in that area that her best chances of employment lay. She defined her target market, quite simply, in the following terms: any corporation or smaller company dealing in chemical and chemical-related products. Her only qualification was, since she wished to travel, that her potential employers be trading on the international market.

3. Maintain Your Campaign Files

Administrators administrate. Rarely do they win top jobs. Seizing that inside campaign track and keeping it depends as much on what you don't do as what you do do. Take record keeping. Establishing campaign files at the very beginning, as dull and as simplistic as the process may seem, will enable you to keep on top of every detail of your effort. Once established, your files can be maintained with an investment in time of less than three minutes a day. Entrepreneurial job hunters win friends and influence people; only pedants and fools *waste* time filing.

Here's what you need to cut through the administrative drudgery of a job hunt:

- An alphabetical card index
- A prospect list file
- A return mail file

Take something as simple as a 3″ × 5″ index card. In isolation, it represents no more than an intelligent means for keeping track of all the prospects you approach, with an ongoing narrative concerning how and when the approach was made and what the consequences of that approach were. But in combination with 100 or 150 more such cards, it becomes part of a compendium of unimaginably useful future professional contacts. Today's card index is tomorrow's list of business acquaintances and friends. The vice-president who interviewed you in March (even though he couldn't make you a job offer) will happily take your call in September when you're working for his competition. A card index, compiled now, will still be working for you in five years' time. Below is a provisional layout for one such card.

Company Name	Prospect's Name
Address	Title
Telephone Number	
	Nature of Contact: Direct Mail
Date of Initial Contact:	: Referral
Follow-up Narrative :	: Headhunter
:	: The Telephone
:	
:	

A prospect list file and a return mail file are no more than adjuncts to your card index. They provide the information upon which it is accurately maintained. The prospect list file is a compiled list of your complete range of prospects. Chances are such a file is going to be messy and unsystematic, since the information it contains will essentially be a collection of notes, letters from business contacts suggesting leads, newspaper clippings, photocopies of directories, and other reference material. The most unpleasant, time-consuming task in your entire job hunt involves organizing this material and transferring the information it contains into your card index.

Your return mail file is more than just a collection of correspondence. It's a databank of psychographic information about every prospect who has responded to your employment approach. The manner in which that return mail is presented, phrased, and signed can tell you whether your prospect is pompous and parochial, energetic and approachable. Check the date of each letter you receive against the date of your original approach. The faster, fresher the response, the more likely your prospect is to be unbureaucratic and on the rise. *That* prospect, even if he deals you a no, might be worth contacting once in a while.

Maintaining campaign files will enable you to stay effortlessly in touch with every nuance in your job-hunting effort. If a prospect calls you, you can flip out the appropriate index card and, in a couple of seconds, remind yourself of who that prospect is, what his responsibilities are, and the manner in which you made the initial contact. You'll come across as confident, crisp, professional. And you will *never* waste an unnecessary moment digging around in piles of disorganized correspondence or other source material when you should be out there talking to the highest bidder.

Case Study: Mary Rose, University Graduate

Mary Rose works for a firm of management consultants. She is an exceptionally career-minded woman who, six months before she was due to graduate from a university in the Midlands of England in the summer of 1973, decided to embark on an elaborate job-hunting campaign. She compiled a list of every management consulting company in Britain: "There were literally hundreds of names on that list," she told us, "but I was determined that every single one of them would know about me."

Having carefully composed her résumé, Mary Rose did a huge mailing to the managing directors of all those consulting firms, a mailing she sent out before organizing their names systematically. Most of her prospects, impressed by her enterprise, wrote back promptly. Some said yes, they would like to see her. Others suggested meetings later in the year. A third group said that, while there were no immediate openings, she should contact them early in the new year when they began their trainee recruitment program. And, of course, she did receive some outright rejections. Responses poured daily through her mailbox. "I didn't know what to do," she said. "I'd developed no systems for sorting out all this return mail. I was overwhelmed. It took me days to get straight, days that might more profitably have been spent following up my most likely prospects." The lesson here is obvious.

Once your campaign gets going, you will be inundated with return mail, return telephone calls, inquiries of various kinds. You are engaged in a professional marketing operation, and professional marketing operations have *consequences*. Trying to track those consequences by reference to that original prospect list file, rather than a card index, will both hinder and confuse your campaign. Worse, it might result in your failing to respond to an important opportunity. Get smart, get organized.

4. Establish Your Mailing Systems

Case Study: Anna Kessler, Research Chemist

A West German research chemist we interviewed was particularly outspoken on several matters relating to the organization of a job hunt. "You have to attack," she insisted. "You have to chase after opportunities quickly and without letting up. But you can only do that if you have the right equipment in a proper state of readiness.

"Consider my situation," she said. "I got my present job as a result of responding to a hot lead on a Saturday evening over drinks with friends. The hiring decision was being made Tuesday, so it was very necessary for me to reach the woman responsible for the decision as quickly as possible.

"Since I'd been looking systematically for a job during the past couple of weeks, I didn't have to think, 'Where the hell am I going to find some decent stationery and a typewriter?' And I didn't compose my job application letter in a panic—I'd already worked all this out. I got up early the next morning and mailed my prospect the hardest-selling letter she'd ever read."

One can forgive Anna's immodesty here because, the fact is, her letter did the trick. The hiring decision was delayed so that an interview with Anna could be squeezed in. "It doesn't matter whether you're setting up an experiment in the laboratory or putting together a job hunt," Anna pointed out. "Failure to complete all the preparatory details can invalidate the entire enterprise."

Tighten up the administrative logic of your mailing systems now, at the outset of your campaign, so you won't have to worry about them later when the pressure is on.

You need: stationery, stamps, carbon paper, and a typewriter. If you can afford it, you really ought to get printed letterhead stationery. It's not particularly expensive, but it looks professional. Your local offset printer (see

"Packaging" for details) will be able to provide it for you at a reasonable price.

Stamps sound obvious. But it's simply amazing how, on the very weekend afternoon when you really feel in the mood to write a couple of special letters to a pair of particularly attractive prospects, the steam goes out of your initiative because, in the back of your mind, the idea pops up that since you have no stamps you can't mail anything until Monday—why bother to write letters now? So, when you make that trip to that grocery store next to the post office, or the bakery next to the post office, or the whatever next to the post office, just pause, get in that interminable post office line, and buy stamps. Lots of them.

The same goes for carbon paper. Needless to say, you won't have a photocopying machine at home. On weekends when you can't surreptitiously use the one in the office, you'll have to be sure you have the means to make a copy of anything you write.

Finally, get hold of a good typewriter with a carbon ribbon and a readable typeface. Don't make do with a machine which produces an uneven, sloppy-looking imprint. As the chapter on "Packaging" explains, everything the female job hunter does should look first-rate. Therefore everything she distributes about herself, excepting the odd personal note, should be typed or printed.

Now you have everything necessary to translate a job-hunting idea onto paper, day or night. You can draft a letter, rephrase a résumé, type an envelope. But don't make a typing error; you forgot to buy correction fluid and it's Sunday and everything's closed.

5. Create Your PR Stance

Anyone selling something to somebody else is in the image business. Appearances count. Especially at a distance, and especially with people you don't know. Add an important extra dimension to your job-hunting campaign by getting a telephone answering service or answering machine. The former is preferable, especially if you can find one that will respond to incoming calls with the use of your name. Not only will an answering service make you appear serious, substantial, and organized, it will also enable you to maintain maximum secrecy about your disaffection for whoever is presently employing you. One tactic to remember when using an answering service is this: since most businesspeople make their major outgoing calls of the day *after* their first cup of coffee and *before* 11 A.M., don't make any lunch dates with friends until you've checked your service at around 11:15. Chances are, nothing much will happen between that time and early afternoon—but don't eliminate the possibility of a job-related luncheon meeting while your campaign is at its height.

6. Analyze Your Costs

Job hunting is expensive. Especially when organized on the scale we recommend. Stay on top of that campaign overhead by budgeting for what you can and cannot afford to spend. Here is a checklist of the main items we believe a sure-fire job hunt requires. For reference purposes we have listed each item under the appropriate section, chapter heading, and subheading.

SECTION	CHAPTER	SUBHEADING	ITEM
Part One	1	Maintain Your Campaign Files	alphabetical card index return mail file (ring binder) prospect list file
		Establish Your Mailing Systems	postage photocopying typewriter (rent, buy, or borrow), or typewriter services

SECTION	CHAPTER	SUBHEADING	ITEM
Part One, Chapter 1 (*continued*)			
		Create Your PR Stance	telephone answering service, or answering machine
Part Two	7	Packaging Your Past: Visual Overview	letterhead: layout, typesetting, and printing envelope: typesetting and printing of return name and address (optional) promotion package: layout, typesetting, and printing
		Packaging Your Personality	clothes and cosmetics
Part Three	10		lunches cabs parking

The total cost of your campaign, if you make use of all the items we include, will not exceed $500. It ought, in fact, to cost a good deal less, since you will be able to borrow rather than buy some of the materials we recommend. Remember, first-class people sell themselves in a first-class fashion. Investing that extra $100 or $150 (especially for clothes) will likely enable you to negotiate a job deal paying a couple of thousand dollars more than it would had you cut budgetary corners.

As a woman we interviewed observed, "If you want a $35,000-a-year job, act and operate as if you deserve it."

2

PLAYING THE PERCENTAGES

THE NAME OF the job-hunting game is numbers, or odds. Recognize this and you are halfway to winning the job you want. Of course, other factors are important too, factors such as how basically saleable you are and how cleverly and appropriately you package and present yourself. But behind these stands a fundamental fact of selling life: the more leads you develop, the greater the likelihood is that you will close the job opportunity you really want.

In marketing, especially mail order or, as it is often called, direct response marketing, a version of playing the percentages is central to the success or failure of every sales campaign. Any book or record club (Book-of-the-Month Club, or Columbia Records and Tapes, for example) that advertises in magazines or on television has a clear understanding of the response levels that each of its advertising efforts will yield. These response levels are analyzed in order to determine how successful they were: first, in terms of the numbers of new sales, or new sales leads, generated; second, in terms of the actual and potential revenues those sales produced. The entire approach is underpinned by the assumption that *for every hundred prospects reached by a particular effort, only a relatively small percentage will respond in a positive way.*

During the course of an interview with a recruitment professional employed by a Montreal-based insurance company, we were given an important insight into how this basic marketing tenet applies to the job hunt. It is to be expected that a large, prestigious corporation will receive job inquiries from many people. What came as a surprise to us was the huge volume of such inquiries: 200 per month, direct to the personnel department, for a corporation employing roughly 7,500 people. Over a twelve-month period, that is equivalent to one-third of the total employee complement of the company—a staggering volume of inquiries. Imagine the competition for attention a résumé has to undergo when it is mailed to a company of 45,000 employees or larger. Every week it would have to compete—relative volumes of incoming mail remaining constant—with about 1,250 other résumés. Our personnel contact said that, regardless of both how exceptional a résumé appeared and how diligently employment inquiries were carried out, "the probability of anyone getting detailed attention is less than they might expect." An understatement, to say the least!*

---

*We recommend in the chapter on "Enemies" that you avoid personnel departments altogether. However, we provide you with these figures to

Our personnel contact went on to say that while, in her opinion, the two vital ingredients for a job hunt were "research and promotion," the scale or size according to which job hunts were conceived was important too. "Think big, but think in terms of percentages," she said. "Think in terms of opening up more leads than you need, not less. That way you'll minimize the risks of failure."

This suggests an important, though frequently overlooked, job-hunting operational rule. The smart job hunter—especially the female job hunter because she has to work harder to get what she wants—has to think, from the very beginning, in terms of *job offers*. Why? Because being offered a job is not the same thing as being hired. As often as not, an offer of employment is made before compensation details—deferred profit sharing, vacations, expense accounts, raises, pension plans—have been discussed. You must understand that you have a lot of hard wheeling and dealing to do in order to negotiate the best possible financial package for yourself. Your hand will be substantially strengthened if you have alternative offers under active consideration and the job offerer knows it. Keep in mind that most job negotiations contain an element of delicacy; *offers can be withdrawn*. Personality conflicts, though not immediately apparent, can arise during the third and fourth meetings. Nuances about your responsibilities, authority, and lines to the top may retard your initial enthusiasm for an offer and cause you to back out.

Operating on the basis of multiple offers has important implications in terms of the size of your original effort. The more offers you want, the more interviews you have to

press home our point that the majority of your prospects won't be offering you a job, one reason obviously being the size of the competition—competition that you can easily rise above.

generate. And the more interviews you want to generate, the larger and more carefully defined must be the size of the initial target market you should be trying to reach.

There is no hard and fast rule about the statistical relationships between the size of your initial target market and the number of interviews an attempt to reach that market will produce. Nor is there a rule about the number of initial interviews necessary to yield a safe and acceptable number of job offers. Direct response marketers, confronted with a version of this same problem, solve it by means of a simple step-by-step approach. In other words, they test. They might, for example, have a total target audience for a particular product of 100,000 prospects. Rather than commit themselves and their money to a one-shot attempt to reach those many prospects they take, say, 10 percent of the total, or even less, and try to reach them. If the results are satisfactory and the response rates fulfill the bottom-line conditions of the promotion, they then expand their effort in order to reach the remainder of the target market. All objective factors staying the same, the logic of their percentage play suggests they will do as well with the remaining portion of their target market as they did in the initial test. For a direct response marketer, the bottom-line conditions are easy to calculate: they are whether an effort makes a profit or loss. For the female job hunter, the bottom-line conditions are tougher to assess: how many offers she needs to generate in order to be very certain that she will win the kind of job she really wants.

Having talked to scores of women about their job-hunting experiences, and having interviewed as many people professionally involved with the recruitment process—headhunters, personnel executives, career advisers—we have come to the conclusion that the number of job offers necessary to land that top position is *three*. Three job offers confer upon you maximum maneuverability in terms of a job negotiation, a wide area of final choice, and reasonable insurance against an unforeseen collapse as you are closing your sale. One offer, in other words, could fall through. Two: well, perhaps. But all three? It's doubtful.

Once the number of offers you should ultimately be aiming for is established, the next step is to ascertain the number of interviews you need to secure those offers. This stage, like the preceding one, involves another percentage play. We asked the president of an executive placement consultancy in Toronto if, in his experience, there was any correlation between the number of interviews a job hunter has and the number of offers those interviews yielded. He said, "Yes. But the correlation isn't precise. If it were, I'd fire all my consultants and rent a computer. Getting a job would simply mean sending each candidate to roughly the same number of interviews. What you have to understand is that the more interviews you have, provided they're with the right kind of people, the better the chances are of getting an offer. That's the correlation."

When pressed, the recruitment consultant added: "A decent candidate, making the right moves in the right direction at the right time, should be able to get *one offer for every ten interviews attended.*"

This conclusion seemed rather optimistic to us, but it will serve as a rule of thumb.

Case Study: Isabel Hughes, Advertising Sales

One of the women with whom we spoke while researching *The Landau Strategy* put together a major job-hunting effort some years ago. It was transcontinental in conception, took three months to execute, and is an object lesson in the logistics of planning.

Isabel Hughes was twenty-five at the time of her campaign, with something of a track record in magazine publishing in Britain. She'd worked originally as a telephone sales executive, selling highly priced subscriptions to various business and academic directories for a small, entrepreneurial publisher in London. After a couple of years she left to join the advertising sales department of a well-known international weekly journal of politics and business. Her job was to sell advertising space to appropriate kinds of advertisers—airlines, trust companies, motor manufacturers, and so forth—in London and in a sales territory in southeast England.

After three years she decided that it would be fun to try to get a job in France, a country in which she had spent part of her childhood and where she still had many friends. The journal for which she was still working had extensive business contacts—there was a European advertising sales department of three—on the Continent and, using the business directories they maintained on file, she was able to identify publishing companies and their senior personnel operating in every major city in France.

Isabel Hughes defined her target market as: business magazines (her specialty) in Paris; consumer magazines in Paris; and, finally, consumer magazines published in other parts of France. The total number of companies she isolated was just under 150; the total number of named individuals at those companies—she was aiming to reach the big guns: publishers, marketing directors, advertising directors—was about 170, since in certain instances she mailed to more than one person at a given magazine.

A cleverly written and presented résumé, a saleable employment history, and an instinctive understanding of the percentage play resulted in her receiving an 8 percent positive response. Of course, she got plenty of polite refusals, and a significant number of those to whom she wrote failed to respond at all. But out of 150 companies that received her résumé, about 12 gave her the chance to talk to them about employment opportunities. In the language of direct marketing, those dozen initial sales leads made the bottom line of her campaign look good. But only in principle. She still had to convert a proportion of those leads into offers. After a ten-day trip to France, Isabel

Hughes managed to eliminate, or was eliminated by, most of her sales leads. "It was frightening in a way," she said, "how quickly those job chances began to evaporate. I thought that with twelve I'd be able to take my pick. In the end I was lucky to get two offers, only one of which I was really enthusiastic about. *Et puis voilà.*"

A number of people with whom we spoke in the recruitment business suggested that somewhere around 10 percent of a job hunter's initial prospects will grant interviews. If the job hunt could be reduced to the level of a predictive science, our analysis would suggest that your target market ought to consist of 300 prospects in order for you to end up with three firm job offers. This is very much an "outside" figure. The more skillfully and precisely you define the prospects within your target market, and the more convincingly you describe and package yourself in a résumé, the less necessary it will be for you to reach such a large number.

Although playing the percentages makes a lot of sense for the average female job hunter, there are circumstances when it is quite inappropriate. For example, the chapter on "The Politics of Promotion" concerns a woman we interviewed who won that top job even though there was only one prospect within her entire target market. She decided, at the outset of her campaign, that since there was just one organization from all those she could choose that really interested her, she would throw all her energy and enterprise into researching that organization and its president. She then built a strategy around everything she could discover about the company and the man who ran it, persuaded him to grant her an interview, and, after a number of other meetings with his subordinates, was finally made a job offer.

We also talked to many other women who secured lucrative positions without having to play the percentages once. They narrowed down their list of prospects to highly manageable numbers (about ten), and put all their efforts into research. With few leads to follow, they developed a detailed level of information about each company. They knew about its directors, growth rates, stock market quotation, and recent corporate acquisitions. They obtained a copy of its annual report (something that requires no more than a telephone call to the public relations department, and a shrewd thing for any job hunter to do before an important interview with a large company) and checked financial newspapers and business magazines for recent reports of each company's activities. Such exhaustive briefing invested all of their employment approaches with considerable authority, an authority their prospects found difficult to resist.

Though personalized approaches can be very effective, the situations when they are appropriate are relatively few. Playing the percentages is a statistically safer strategy. Whichever one you decide to adopt, remember this: neither will work effectively unless it is founded upon diligent research into the identification of your target market and, above all, an understanding of how to reach it once it has been identified.

And that brings us to the crucial issue of media.

3

MEDIA

MARKETING IS NEITHER
quite art, nor quite science.
It seems to hover uncertainly between the two disciplines.
On the one hand, it's management by objectives; on the
other, it's inspired improvisation. The most formidable
marketers understand this, accept it, and spend their time
making cool, calculated transitions between the two extremes. You, the top job hunter, must too.

Consider the idea, introduced earlier, that the name of
the job-hunting game is numbers, or odds. It's an important, though ultimately incomplete notion: job hunting by
pocket calculator. Unquestionably, the indiscriminate use

of numbers alone is not enough. You have to *reach* those prospects within your target market accurately and in the most suitable manner. Where, for want of drama and direction, the percentage play falls short, media come in.*

You have at your disposal an armory of media options that will enable you to reach your prospects with the same precision as the marketing professionals. The only difference is that your media devices are a shade unconventional, and rather small in scale. Job hunters have, we think, no more than four primary media options at their disposal through which to reach their target market:

1. Direct Mail
2. Referrals
3. Headhunters
4. The Telephone

There are, of course, other options open to you; options like going to employment agencies, or answering recruitment advertisements in the newspapers, or even perhaps running classified ads on your own behalf in newspapers or trade periodicals. As far as the last option is concerned, we think it's a waste of time. Important prospects do not look at the classified columns of newspapers when they want to fill a top job. The trouble with the other two is that they are essentially defensive. They oblige you to wait for opportunities to arise, rather than allowing you to find them yourself. Job opportunities fall into two categories:

Media is a word that can be understood in at least two ways. Most people think of it as a generic term denoting a loose alliance of left-leaning nihilists working in the communications industry, as in the expression "the media." Others think of it more technically, as a word describing that wide range of devices society uses to disseminate information: television and radio, newspapers and magazines, billboards and direct mail. Marketing professionals most frequently use the word in this latter sense.

those that are waiting to be filled, and those that are created to accommodate an outstanding candidate. The media options we recommend enable you to attack that vital second category of opportunities as well as the first.

Needless to say, the four primary media options isolated here are neither unique nor unusual. They are the kinds of devices most intelligent women on the job market would consider adopting to get through to potential employers. The trouble is that women unschooled in their use inevitably make certain elementary mistakes about them. They apply them haphazardly. Or they use just one of them to the exclusion of the rest. Through ignorance, job hunters scatter direct mail so crudely that they alienate more prospects than they persuade. They telephone a prospect directly when that prospect should have been sent a personal letter. Or they send a glossy promotion package to someone who could have been sold by the use of a referral. The message of this chapter is: smart top-job hunters, like shrewd marketing professionals, never try to sell the *right* prospect through the *wrong* media device.

1. Direct Mail

Fast and flexible, direct mail is to the job hunter what an accurate throwing arm is to the star quarterback. With direct mail you can transmit the right message, at the right time, in the right format, to the right prospect. The vocabulary of hunting has provided direct mail marketers with one of their most vital tactical distinctions: the difference between "shotgun" and "rifle" mailings. Of the two concepts the former suggests dispersal, the latter precision. The canny job hunter must understand, and master, both.

Shotguns are for blasting. "Fast and dirty," as the pros would say, a shotgun mailing is one that enables you to reach large numbers of prospects in your target market with a promotional message that, though composed and packaged with linguistic flair and visual tact, is basically a standard one. An ingenious time-saver, this kind of mailing lets you get away with writing only two or three letters and then having the texts offset printed. Clearly, if you have isolated (like some of the people in the case studies we have already described) 150 or more prospects in your target market who could most appropriately be reached through the mail, it would be folly to try to write personal letters to each of them. The smart job hunter recognizes that and makes the quintessential percentage play—zapping prospects with waves of mail.

A well-written, well-designed shotgun mailing can be enormously successful (often yielding a 10–15 percent response) and it's particularly satisfying to watch those responses pouring daily through your mailbox. It's a terrific morale booster!

Rifles: long, lean, and hard, they're a promoter's dream. A rifle mailing is the job hunter's deadliest media weapon. The approach is most effectively used to reach probably no more than twenty-five prospects with material specifically written to relate your background and experience to each of those prospects' interests and needs. In other words, there's no shortcut here—you have to write individual letters.

Though time-consuming, rifle mailings almost always yield higher response rates than shotgun mailings. In selling, the personal approach outperforms the impersonal one. Making prospects *feel you care* can have dramatic consequences. The rifle mailing is the promotion equivalent of a long, questing look in your prospect's eye. That prospect (especially if he has had a tough climb to the top) will respect an extra effort and, even if there are no top jobs going, might give you a helping hand.

Case Study: Sharon Hunt, Hotel Management

Sharon was an administrative assistant working for a prominent hotel group in New York. After completing a special training course in hotel administration, she decided to try to get herself a better position elsewhere in the industry. Sales oriented, entrepreneurial, and single, she was prepared to work hard and go anywhere to learn the hotel business.

She analyzed her target market carefully and identified a total of eighty prospects in the following employment categories: (1) the highly prestigious, independent hotels, such as the Ritz-Carltons of Boston and Montreal; (2) the major international hotel chains, like Sheraton and Western International.

She decided each of her two categories of hotels required a different approach. "I figured," she told us, "that the independent hotels would be the ones most likely to respond to a personal approach. The others, the big chains, I could handle more loosely."

Sharon mailed the general manager of each of the fifteen hotels in her first category a personal two-page letter, one that incorporated the highlights of her background and experience and related them very specifically to what she hoped were that hotel's business interests and objectives. The remaining sixty-five hotels (category 2) were sent her résumé with a standard letter whose text she marginally varied, depending on the character of the group she was approaching.

This division of her effort exemplifies the difference between the shotgun and rifle approaches to mailing. The rifle tactic works best when you are aiming, as we said, at a target market of no more than twenty-five prospects. Trying to write personally to more people than that is pure drudgery. The shotgun tactic is most effective when you want to reach significant numbers of prospects, especially when copy prefabrication is adopted.* The shotgun tactic, as we have argued, is perfect for a percentage play.

"I got great results from my personal letter," Sharon said, "far more than with my more general mailing. Although, when I analyzed it, the total number of interview offers worked out to roughly the same. I got eight interviews from my personal letter, nine from the general effort. The percentage return was different, that's all."

Media-wise professional marketers mix their direct mail strategies. Media-smart female job hunters should, too.

2. Referrals

The circumspect person likes referrals. They're personal, proper, neat, and tidy. Potentially, they're a powerful media option for the female job hunter. And they're cheap. It costs you next to nothing to reach prospects within your target market on the basis of a recommendation.

Case Study: Elizabeth Kaufmann, Data Processing

"Referrals are political."

So said Elizabeth Kaufmann, a woman we met on vacation and persuaded to reminisce about her job-hunting campaign that took place a couple of years earlier in Zurich. "By saying that," she went on, "I mean that an interview can very much be influenced in your favor when it is organized through a referral. Especially if that referral is well known and respected."

Elizabeth pointed out that Swiss society is dominated by a deep respect for life's underlying proprieties. Add to

---

*Copy prefabrication is a technique which enables you to compose promotional material (especially letters) around prewritten, interchangeable blocks of copy; copy that, though created according to the time-saving standards of the assembly line, actually reads as if it were personalized. "Language" includes a case study (Jacqueline Casey) which illustrates in more detail the advantages and logistics of this procedure.

that the sensitive, secretive character of a high technology, innovative industry like data processing, and you have a situation in which job changing needs to be undertaken with maximum caution and finesse. And referrals add that necessary touch of finesse. They break the ice. Whomever you use as an intermediary creates, by virtue of his or her involvement, an atmosphere of informality and trust between you and your interviewer.

"My key referral contact was the president of the association representing data processing," Elizabeth continued, observing parenthetically that most professions, from marketing to journalism, have such associations— associations whose senior executive staff are well connected and generally possess a higher than average enthusiasm for the business they are in. These people can usually be counted on to be helpful to fellow professionals looking for career leads. "I went to see the president, told him about my background, and asked for help. He offered it willingly, supplying names and telephone numbers and hints—though he made it clear that in so doing he was in no way endorsing me. Of course I understood that the mere fact of being able to use his name as an introduction was enormously helpful: the endorsement was *implied*, not *declared*. But it was still an endorsement."

In pursuing the referral leads with which she had been provided by her initial contact, Elizabeth found that they snowballed rapidly. Early prospects, even if they had no opportunities to discuss with her, themselves became referral sources, thus enabling Elizabeth's referral momentum to continuously build.

"Within a week I had compiled a master file of twenty top men and women whom I could confidently approach, almost always using the name of someone they knew as an introduction. In a sense I became a member of *their* club. *Verstehen?*"

Illuminating though Elizabeth Kaufmann's story is,

the female job hunter should recognize that a referral strategy has its weaknesses too. For one thing, referrals are both limited and limiting. It's hard to reach large numbers of prospects within your target market this way. So if you're making a percentage play, referrals can have only a restricted role in your overall campaign strategy.

Referrals can be time-wasting and depressing. Prospects may agree to see you out of courtesy to your go-between, not because they are genuinely interested in you. The courtesy meeting set up through the help of a friend can, undertaken with sufficient frequency, be devastating to your morale.

Referrals can backfire. An inappropriate request for a referral can put the best of business acquaintanceships under unnecessary strain.

And referrals leak. Word can easily get back to your current employer that you've got itchy feet. Unless you are trying to up the ante with your present company, run your referral operation very carefully.

As with direct mailing, so with referrals. There are two kinds, each of which requires different treatment:

Active Referrals

Active referrals are go-betweens. They agree to talk favorably about you to those prospects in your target market whom they know. They sell you without your having to sell yourself—perfect for those with a nervous disposition.

Passive Referrals

Passive referrals are the type that Elizabeth Kaufmann used so effectively. They allow you to use their name as a means of gaining the attention of prospects, but do no more than that. While they may recommend you, they won't actively sell you.

3. Headhunters

Using headhunters, that group of operators in the job market who specialize in so-called management or executive recruitment, as a media device is, perhaps, our most controversial and questionable recommendation. For it is usually they who use the job hunter—to meet the personnel requirements of their corporate clientele. Handle headhunters with kid gloves. While they offer an attractive additional means of opening up employment opportunities for, and at no expense to, the job hunter, unless they're owned and run by women with strong feminist inclinations, they can't be relied upon to deal with women entirely on the level. That is especially true when it comes to the details of financial compensation.

Women, remember, are traditionally paid less than men for comparable work. Headhunters can normally be expected to take advantage of this reality if it means making a placement, despite the fact that it can cut into the size of their fee. Our suggestion? Simple. Manipulate the manipulators. Use them; don't let them use you. The following case study shows you how.

Case Study: Susan Peterson, Account Management

Susan Peterson first recognized the potential of headhunters about eighteen months after having joined an advertising agency as a trainee. "I was working in the media department of the agency at the time," she explained, "and felt that, though media work was intriguing, it was insufficiently creative for me. Having decided to look for another job, it struck me that I should try to apply what I had been learning professionally to the problems connected with my job hunt. *I sat down and analyzed my media options.* I considered the usual alternatives. You know, the mail, and through contacts. I knew pretty much where I'd like to work but, being new to the business, I didn't know a great deal about who had hiring authority for someone like me. Nor, incidentally, did I know how much I was worth. For these two reasons, I decided to use a headhunter. Then the thought occurred to me that perhaps the smart thing to do was call up the personnel departments of the ad agencies that interested me and ask them which outside recruitment consultants they used. All I had to do then was contact the consultants they named and suggest that they might want to try selling me to their client.''

It worked. She had a new job within six weeks.

Encouraged by this strategy that had performed well for her five years earlier, she used a slightly modified version of it when changing jobs again. She simply put her name forward to the best-connected headhunter in the advertising agency business, told the headhunter she was on the job market, indicated the companies for which she'd like to work, and authorized the headhunter to make the appropriate inquiries. Susan Peterson's track record and the fact that a person of her caliber was available could be counted on to inspire more than average interest among potential employers. Although this tactic worked for Susan a second time, it is not advised for a woman without something fairly impressive in the way of professional achievement behind her.

Headhunters play a crucial supporting media role in any job-hunting campaign. The trick is to determine, ahead of time, the number of prospects within your target market who you feel could be most suitably reached by using them. Take a sample of your total prospects, and test the effectiveness of headhunters as a means of getting you a potentially profitable interview. If they succeed, encourage them with more leads. If they don't, you still have three other media options working for you meanwhile—direct mail, referrals, and the telephone.

4. The Telephone

The telephone is an instrument of business much taken for granted. One of modern marketing's most powerful media devices, it is used to sell a wide range of merchandise, everything from magazine subscriptions to electronic equipment. On the purely social level, effective use of the telephone requires no special competence. But the use of the telephone to present a business proposition is something else again. Handled with confidence and authority, the telephone can be not only the most effective but also the cheapest option in the job hunter's entire media armory. Handled improperly, the telephone can destroy a promising employment opportunity in seconds.

The first thing to understand is that the telephone is a corporate status symbol of considerable potency. Middle-echelon businessmen with upper-echelon aspirations use the telephone to elevate themselves and their work. They rarely dial their own outside calls, or personally accept an incoming call; a secretary does it for them. And "hold" is the supreme aphrodisiac: nothing gives them a bigger thrill than keeping an importunate stranger, especially an importunate female stranger, dangling by that sensual electronic thread. There is a simple rule governing the influence of the prospect you are trying to reach with your telephone call: the more screening you encounter, the more likely your prospect is to be weak. Powerful people pick up their own phones.

In general, we don't recommend the use of the telephone as a means of initiating employment opportunities. Except in certain areas of sales, prospects tend to be alienated when called cold. Still, the telephone can be profitably used in the context of a passive referral; that is, when a third party has allowed you to mention his or her name as an introduction. Mostly, though, the telephone will be a follow-up device.

It may be, however, that you are particularly effective on the telephone (just as others are outstanding at face-to-face meetings, while still others write marvelous-sounding letters), in which case you might definitely consider employing the telephone more aggressively. Should you decide to use it, either for passive referrals or for straight cold calling, *test it first*. Take 5 or 10 percent of your total prospects and assess how well or how badly the telephone works for you. If more than 20 percent of the people you call agree enthusiastically to see you, then by all means use the telephone more frequently; it's the fastest and cheapest of your media options. But if you seem to be turning people off, eliminate the telephone entirely from your media armory; use it only as a follow-up device.

When using the telephone remember to:

- Prepare a casual, to-the-point introduction for the moment when you get your prospect on the line.

  One woman we met totally froze as she was making her opening remarks to a high-profile, exceptionally powerful female executive whom a referral suggested she call. What happened was that her referral gave her the woman's *direct dial* number. So instead of getting through to the switchboard and then a secretary (creating a delay which would have allowed her to collect herself), the phone rang once and was answered instantly in an authoritative fashion by the executive herself. The young careerist felt a paralyzing surge of stage fright run down her spine and heard herself sputter the only words her stunned speech mechanism could manage to bring forth: "Oh. Er. Hi. Gee." A prepared speech, however informal, would have saved her a great deal of embarrassment. Use one.
- Write out an informal script for the occasions when, unavoidably, you will be asked to talk about yourself and your accomplishments to an unfamiliar prospect.

  In general, of course, it's far better to hold out for a

person-to-person meeting if you want to persuade someone to hire you, but don't be afraid to discuss your career objectives on the telephone. Read your script as if you were being forced to think aloud. Throw in some hesitations, the odd rhetorical question, and several pauses as if you were remembering. Your prospect will be impressed with how articulately you extemporize. He might even suggest a meeting.

- Identify yourself immediately by name on all calls.
- If your prospect is unavailable, refuse to get sidetracked by a secretary. Ask politely but firmly when your prospect will be available to take a call from you.
- Address your prospect by name throughout the conversation.
- Express a courtesy request, e.g., "Do you have a moment to talk?" Talk slowly, at conversational speed. The recommended speech rate for telephone sales personnel is 150 words per minute. To assess your word rate, take a 750-word article and read it aloud. It should take five minutes. Practice.
- Introduce the name of your referral (if this is the context in which you are placing the call) and the circumstances through which that referral is known to you.

You might use one of the following opening remarks.

A. "I called X the other day and X suggested I call you."
B. "I was talking to X the other day and X suggested I call you."
C. "X and I were chatting the other day and X suggested I call you."
D. "During the meeting I had with X the other day, X suggested I call you."
E. "I had lunch/dinner/a drink with X the other day, and X suggested I call you."

These remarks, each of which is progressively more intimate, convey the nature of your relationship with your passive referral. A and B suggest a sense of distant formality; C and E imply that you and your referral are on close terms; and D suggests that you have a prior business relationship with your referral. Only you can decide which of these openers you should use. You can probably think of a dozen others. We believe it's better to hint at the closest possible relationship between you and your contact consistent with the truth, and it's even acceptable to somewhat exaggerate that closeness (businesspeople do it all the time) rather than play it down. You are selling something, after all.

- Tell your prospect why you are making the approach.
- Don't outstay your welcome. It's an axiom of telephone selling that the moment your prospect has agreed to buy—in your case, agreed to a meeting—you quickly, pleasantly, bring the conversation to an end. The name of the game is "Close and Go."
- Smile when you dial. Sounds corny but, believe it or not, smiling helps. A smile sends a psychic shock wave down those telephone wires right to the heart of your prospect. You'll feel better about each other.

Adopt a high-octane media strategy in your job-hunting campaign. Be flexible, improvise, experiment. Identify the total number of prospects in your target market and try to reach them through a controlled combination of *all four* media options.* If you have 100 prospects in your target market, make a discretionary judgment about

---

*Chapter 8, "The Launch," contains the Campaign Execution Schedule that allows you to handle your media options so they work at maximum efficiency and effectiveness.

how best to break them down into manageable groups. Attack 50, say, with a combination of shotgun and rifle mail; reach 15 via referrals; 15 more with the aid of head-hunters; and 20 with cold telephone calls.

The top marketing professional is scrupulous when it comes to establishing the statistical structure of a media campaign. And for a simple reason: once the parameters of the plan are established, the pressure's off. *That* is absolutely the secret of ulcer-proof media planning. Get the numbers right. Get the media options set up. Press the start button. A properly designed, fully operational media strategy in your job-hunting campaign should give you plenty of scope to be creative and have fun.

Marketing is, ultimately, an exercise in manipulation. At the height of your campaign, provided you are tracking your responses accurately, you will have plenty of opportunities for, as the direct marketing boys would say, "massaging the numbers." Don't be shy. Play the media game for all it's worth. Of all the job-hunting campaign games in town, it's the one most likely to succeed.

4

ENEMIES

THE JOB HUNT is a kind of guerrilla warfare. Especially for women. Success comes to those who know how to exploit cover, negotiate unpleasant terrain, interpret the complex and often juvenile geography of the corporate hiring process. For women in the top-job market, talent all too often has to take a back seat to stealth and circumspection. Beyond her sexual disadvantage in an area of life dominated and defined by men, the female job hunter also has to take account of the objective hazards common to any serious job-hunting campaign.

Job hunters, male and female, have enemies. Female

job hunters just have more of them. It's as simple as that. Here, we think, are potentially the most malign:

1. Personnel departments
2. Headhunters
3. The photocopying machine
4. Mothers
5. Career counselors
6. Friends
7. Gimmicks
8. You

1. Personnel Departments

"We're the enemy," said a personnel executive in a substantial North American pharmaceutical company. "We don't hire. The line managers do that, or the departmental managers, or vice-presidents. We get in the way—that's our function. Don't write to us if you want a job. Write to the person who can hire you."

It's all there—realism about the essentially obstructive function of the personnel bureaucracy, at least as far as it affects recruitment. It's not that personnel people want to be obstructive; it's simply that, by the very nature of their work, they have to be.

If there is a common thread running through the discussions we've had with successful—and not so successful—female job hunters, it is this: personnel departments are the quintessential graveyard in which so many job-hunting efforts are laid to rest. Some women we've met have quite rightly observed that if they were asked to discuss an employment opportunity with someone in personnel, they would be offended. However, these were exceptional women negotiating substantial positions, the technical natures of which people in personnel departments could not be expected to understand. It may be that you will be asked to meet a personnel executive preparatory to talking to a higher-up. That's unavoidable. The message that we want to get across here is that it's folly to make your initial contact with a company through personnel.

As the chapter "Playing the Percentages" showed, personnel departments are characteristically overwhelmed with unsolicited résumés, so the chance that yours will get individual attention is relatively small. In addition, personnel departments are frequently the last to know of any employment opportunities within their own company. And, since they stand at the bottom rung of most corporate hierarchies, their influence on hiring decisions is marginal at best. They may screen candidates, but that's it.

What's more, personnel departments are a bureaucracy, and bureaucracies move slowly. By the time your résumé has been considered, sent to the various relevant departments for review, returned, and chewed over some more, weeks will have passed. And that's no good.

2. Headhunters

The trouble with headhunters—and it's the reason they have to be regarded as an enemy—is that their allegiance is to the company by whom they are compensated, rather than to the individual job seeker whose experience and talent they are trying to promote. Despite their sanctimonious denials of any similarity to the more proletarian employment agencies, both groups (with few exceptions) make their money in the same way: through finder's fees or progressive payments from the companies that retain them. This means that, since their financial well-being is dependent upon their corporate clients rather than upon you, their primary concern will be to keep *them* happy. Any woman and, for that matter, any man contemplating the use of such organizations should keep this in mind.

For women, though, there are special dangers. Like most smart businesspeople, headhunters, unless they are blessed with inordinate integrity, will always take the line of least resistance in order to make their sale. Talented women can offer them extra leverage in one important respect; as job candidates they enable the headhunter to whisper, *sotto voce*, to his client: "Got a great gal here. And you can get her for less than that other guy you saw."

Headhunters are also used by unscrupulous companies who have no intention of hiring a woman but for legal reasons must pretend to be considering candidates of both sexes for a particular position. A woman can then end up going to a token interview with a headhunter in order to make that headhunter's chauvinist client appear unprejudiced.

You would do well, therefore, to search out feminist-owned and operated agencies which can be relied upon to give you a fair shake. Failing that, you have only limited alternatives, the most compelling of which is the use of headhunters to reach those prospects in which you have established a prior interest. This tactic enables you to control the headhunter rather than allowing the headhunter to control you. It's a particularly effective device if you are operating with maximum secrecy in your job search and you decide to use a headhunter as a discreet go-between.

One final tip: you should never tell a headhunter what you are making in your present job. Chances are it's lower—probably a good deal lower—than the salary of a comparable male. Rather, tell the headhunter what you expect to make. If pressed, don't admit the truth about your current salary. Add 20 or 30 percent to the figure and let it go at that. There's nothing immoral in this tactic. If, as is extremely unlikely, you are challenged over what, after all, is an untruth, calmly outface it. Quote government figures, salary statistics, anything that supports your view that women are always paid less generously than men, and add that you see no reason that you should perpetuate an outmoded trend.

3. The Photocopying Machine

The photocopying machine is a fast, accurate device for reproducing written material. You will use it frequently during your job hunt: to copy source material, lists, letters. That's fine. But never make the mistake of supposing that a photocopy is anything other than stale. A photocopied résumé sent to a prospect is doomed. It says that you have not made an original effort; that he or she is just one among many potential employers that you are trying to reach.

Everything you present on paper during your campaign must be crisp, clear, and compelling; photocopies are out in every circumstance except the most routine.

4. Mothers

Mothers are bad news for the aggressive, career-minded working woman. Why? (Your mother may be an exception to this observation, but we doubt it.) Because mothers, when it comes to their daughters (not their sons), are given to issuing overprotective, defeatist advice. Enslaved by the tired social proprieties of a generation dedicated to the notion that men go out and do things while women stay home stirring soup and giving birth, mothers can rarely be counted on to give their blessing to a major career initiative that, by implication, calls into question their own domestic achievements. We are, of course, not alone in holding this view. Not only is it a major intellectual point of departure for a dozen feminist polemics, it is also a proposition supported by carefully researched academic texts.

Interestingly, *The Managerial Woman*, that brilliant book by Margaret Hennig and Anne Jardim (every serious working woman should read it, twice) explores, among other things, the cultural influences that tend to define and constrain the career options open to women and the manner in which women pursue them. One of Hennig's and Jardim's findings concerns the effects mothers have on the attitudes and aspirations of their daughters, especially during childhood and adolescence, and, in particular, how mothers condition their daughters to see only the negative consequences of chance-taking. During their daughters' upbringing, mothers emphasize the cost of failure in risk-taking; they overlook the positive consequences of the successful gamble. In addition, especially during their daughters' adolescence, mothers sell the so-called traditional roles designated for women—marriage, children, the home—at the expense of options which, mothers believe, are more appropriately pursued by their sons.

All this has destructive consequences for the attitude so many women bring to their own career advancement.

Our advice is, unless your mother is very exceptional, keep her out of your latest career maneuver. Tell your dad. He'll probably give you good advice, and might even make a contribution to your promotion budget. But swear him to secrecy.

5. Career Counselors

While we entertain certain ambiguous feelings about headhunters—sometimes they're useful, sometimes they're sharks—we entertain almost no ambiguous feelings whatsoever about career counselors or career advisers or executive development specialists or whatever they call themselves. Any organization advertising the fact that, for a fee, it will help you analyze your career objectives, prepare your résumé, advise you on interview strategy, and, ultimately, get you a job, is almost certainly useless and probably corrupt. Many of these outfits, regardless of whether they get you a job or not, charge up to $3,000 for their professional services, which, with some imagination and common sense, most job seekers can develop for themselves.

The ratio of bad publicity to good that these organizations have received is overwhelming, and it's hard to find a job-hunting handbook that has anything agreeable to say about them. In his book *What Color Is Your Parachute?* Richard Nelson Bolles, who demolishes such companies with convincing finality, observes that senior officers from one of the largest such firms, Frederick Chusid & Co., testified during a civil suit brought against the company before its bankruptcy in 1974 that only between 30 and 40 percent of its clients during the previous six months had succeeded in getting a new job. Those clients that didn't, still had to pay.

Although, of course, there are legitimate operators in career counseling, the chances are that they won't, even if they are any good, have a great deal of professional expertise in the areas of difficulty that women characteristically confront in their job hunt. So, unless you're very confident of being placed by one of these companies, because it comes highly recommended by someone you trust, put your money to better use.

6. Friends

There is an important distinction between "friends" and "friends in the business." Those consoling, supportive, wonderful people who fall into the first category are beyond reproach in most things you do in life. Except when you're on a job hunt. Under no circumstances allow them to participate, especially when it comes to setting you up with interviews. The courtesy meeting arranged through the benevolent intercession of a pal represents not only a waste of time but also, attended in sufficient numbers, a major route to discouragement and loss of morale. Unless your friends are particularly well connected in an employment field that directly interests you, keep them out of your search.

7. Gimmicks

The promotion business—which your job-hunting campaign should, in part at least, exemplify—is riddled with gimmicks of various kinds. People are prepared to go to outlandish lengths to sell themselves and/or their products. But job acquisition is not an area appropriate to the bizarre oversell. The thought may have occurred to you that a mass distribution by air of your résumé printed on monogrammed notepaper might well be instrumental in helping you win that top job. It won't.

One personnel director to whom we spoke showed us the résumé of a woman who had painstakingly mounted a full-color photograph of herself—she was attractive—on a 4″ × 6″ card, the reverse side of which contained a brief account of her accomplishments and career ambitions. The personnel director held the flyer delicately between the thumb and forefinger of his right hand and passed it to us for our inspection. "My entire department loved this," he said. "Loved it. But that's all."

Even in the promotion game, there's a fine distinction between gimmickry and flair. The gimmick is frequently perceived as a species of larceny, while flair is, quite rightly, connected with independence of mind.

Everything you do in your job hunt, from writing a

follow-up letter to presenting yourself for a luncheon meeting with a possible employer, should exhibit you as bright, energetic, spirited, willing to learn, agreeable. You may, at heart, have the instincts of a hustler. That's not necessarily a bad thing. Just try not to let them surface—especially during an important interview.

8. You

The job hunt, like travel, is a form of introspection. It is intensely self-revealing. You will be subjected, especially if the job offer you seek is as important, powerful, and well paid as you feel you deserve, to intense personal scrutiny. Such professional weaknesses that you have, unless you are enormously careful, will be systematically called into question. Your capacity for sloppy thinking, cowardice, narcissism, and plain stupidity—characteristics that you have carefully concealed over the years, even from yourself—will be mercilessly exposed. You will learn that in a business meeting every inflection counts. The wrong word expressed at the wrong time can, at a stroke, destroy a week of preparation; a misjudged attempt to be overfamiliar can result in your being perceived as a coquette.

You will try to press for an advantage in an interview situation where none exists; you will allow yourself to be manipulated onto the defensive (especially in a salary negotiation) when you should have been aggressive and even cavalier. You will occasionally fail to respond to opportunities with sufficient speed, to dress in a manner that properly reflects the business environment in which you are trying to sell yourself; you will fail to maintain your campaign files efficiently, so that you flounder and fuss at an unexpected incoming call one evening from a corporate VP who was fascinated by your résumé and who naturally expects you to know who he is and what he does (you wrote him a cleverly personalized letter, one of 150, re-member?) and who is surprised when you hem and haw and generally behave like an ill-prepared moron—which is what, at that moment, you are, and *he* knows it.

Yes, in a job hunt, you are potentially the gravest, most committed enemy you will encounter. And for a simple reason: because every mistake you make is *your* mistake. You can't blame the other members of your department because you *are* the department. You are planner, media coordinator, copywriter, promotion strategist, negotiator. If there is a single lesson to be learned from this book it is this: top jobs are won (and lost) by candidates, not em-ployers. This observation may be tough to take, particu-larly when set against the impossibility of circumventing stiff-necked, implacable male prejudice. But in taking it you will be thrown back foursquare on your own resources which are, in the last analysis, the only things standing between yourself and mediocrity.

Your campaign now has a sense of purpose and direc-tion. Despite the fact that you have neither made a job-hunting telephone call nor distributed a single résumé, the foundations for a major promotion have been exhaustively laid. You have analyzed your objectives, defined your target market, developed your media options, and estab-lished your basic administrative systems.

Now you have to confront a second major task: the development of the promotion itself. Relax. Repeat to yourself, like a mantra, "I have to plan my sale, promote my sale, make my sale." Of the three stages, the second is tougher than the first, the third tougher than the second. You still have a long way to go.

PART TWO
PROMOTION

5

THE POLITICS
OF PROMOTION
A CASE STUDY IN
PRESIDENTIAL
AUTHORITY*

GETTING A JOB is striking a bargain. That bargaining process begins not during the first ten seconds of an interview but now, as you enter the promotion stage of your campaign: the manner in which you promote your sale

---

*We are indebted to Professor Richard E. Neustadt, author of *Presidential Power*, for a number of ideas expressed in this chapter. Though Professor Neustadt's book dealt with, and was in a sense dedicated to, the realities of presidential power in the White House, many of his insights are relevant to the job hunt.

will determine the terms upon which you will be allowed to bargain to make that sale later.

We have two things to say in this chapter. First, women on the job hunt have to learn to aim high. Don't waste time with departmental underlings or minor divisional managers unless you are certain that they carry clout in the corporate hiring process. Corporation presidents are often the *most accessible* individuals in their entire company. Don't be afraid to make a direct employment approach to them. Second, try to understand that promoting your sale and making your sale are intimately connected: the moment you reach your prospect for the first time you are making an opening bid in a negotiation that might take weeks. Promote your sale *as* a professional *to* professionals.

We have subtitled this chapter "A Case Study in Presidential Authority" because it contains a fascinating example of a female job hunter who won the position she was after as a consequence of some smart maneuvering at the highest possible corporate level. Aiming high, she won that top job. If you have any doubt about the hiring power of the prospect you've selected to receive your résumé, distribute it instead to the vice-president or president to whom that prospect reports.

We are not suggesting here that *every* employment approach you make should be at the presidential level. A particular vice-president or divisional manager in, for example, a company about which you have reliable information may be an ideal target for your résumé. What frequently happens when a company president receives an interesting and unusual résumé is that the president replies directly to you, recommending that you get in touch with an alternative person in his organization whom the president may well have enthusiastically advised of your interest.

Presidents are powerful; everything that so many middle managers are not! They can usually be counted on to be courteous, prompt, and helpful. They are rarely interested in scoring cheap points off ambitious women. On the contrary, being older, and usually male, they tend to be rather paternalistic. And, of course, their every gesture is laden with the power and authority of their office. Presidents, unlike middle managers (who are often preoccupied with trivial little departmental power struggles having to do with their own immediate interests), usually take the larger, corporate view. Intense self-interest may have secured them their job in the first place, but they will inevitably have mellowed by the time they are anointed president. They become rabbinical, judicious, and somewhat sober. And, most important of all, company presidents are still predominantly male, a fact that women may as well turn to their advantage by making use of men's natural predisposition to like them; especially those women who have the good sense to make a highly professional appeal to their fundamental business interests.

Those interests, incidentally, are quite easy to identify because they are the bedrock upon which all efficient businesses must be built. There are three of them:

1. a recognition of the need to make a profit
2. a belief in a reward system that compensates achievement and punishes, or at least frowns upon, failure
3. a commitment to growth, if not in size, then in sales

Case Study: Ellen Forbes, Publishing

Ellen Forbes was an editor in one of the book divisions of a large British publishing house. However, Britain was beginning to bore her, so she decided to move to the United States.

Through the North American contacts she had made over the years, she was able to identify several book publishing companies in New York that interested her, but only one whose activities were sufficiently extensive in the subjects which she knew best, sociology and political science. Playing the percentages would obviously be inappropriate in her case.

It so happened that she was already on good, but inevitably distant, terms with a couple of people working in the firm. Both were in an excellent position to offer her informed advice about the company's operations and management, and the personalities and professional predispositions of the senior people who ran it. In particular, she was anxious to find out as much as she could about the president. She made inquiries about his background, his career moves, his instincts about the industry, and his business reputation. As she said, "If presidents like you, the chances are vice-presidents will as well. And if vice-presidents like you, divisional managers will too. In any hierarchy, those below always try hard to go along with the preferences of those above them. Often their jobs depend on it."

As a keen student of politics and political theory, Ellen Forbes had developed certain insights about the tactics of persuasion in the context of government institutions; now she had the chance to apply those insights to the job hunt. Her problem, and her challenge, was this: to "read" that single, particular prospect in her target market so shrewdly that, with his help (which in this context meant the help of his *presidential* power), she could sell herself into the editorial position she sought.

Having learned all she could of the president, she then began to develop the text of a letter that she planned to send him. The letter was designed to do a number of things. First, to tell her prospect about those of her achievements and skills in book publishing that were directly relevant to what she understood to be his professional preoccupations and needs. Second, to suggest the ways in which she might be able to help expand and improve the publishing activities of the division that interested her, and thereby increase its capacity to sell books. Third, to appeal, in the overall style and presentation of her letter, to what she had discovered to be her prospect's exceptional fastidiousness. Finally, to time her approach in such a way that the chances of his wanting to meet her were at their greatest.*

The letter was mailed in the middle of April and contained the announcement that she was planning to be in New York "sometime in June," a vagueness that would enable her to modify her travel plans in accordance with his availability. She invited her prospect to suggest a convenient day for a meeting.

He did so. Replying in classic business style, he observed that although there were no "immediate openings" her letter "impressed and intrigued" him. He suggested they get together the third week of June.

They met in his office at 5:15 one evening. The manner in which her initial contact had been made was reciprocated by the person at whom it was aimed. She was given ample opportunity to explain her case. At no time was she asked hostile, searching questions, although she was well prepared to defend herself against them should they have arisen. On the contrary, her prospect did most of the talking. He told her about how his company was run and what its growth objectives were. He discussed the weaknesses and strengths of the division which she had expressed a desire to join. The president treated her as his equal: equal in terms of accomplishment, insight, and ambition.

At the end of a pleasant hour he observed that although there were no jobs available in the division under discussion, he felt strongly that she should still meet with the division's editorial director, in order to explore future possibilities.

---

*See "The Launch" for a discussion on timing.

"The moment he said that he felt strongly I should speak to the person who ran the division, I knew I was in with a chance," she explained. Her reasoning was simple. At a stroke, the president had invested all her subsequent meetings with other staff members with a portion of the power, status, and authority of his office. If someone down the hierarchy felt inclined to offer her a job, even if the offer should involve a risk (such as, for example, exceeding a departmental budget), that person could be confident of *endorsing a prior presidential judgment* and being, to that extent, *invulnerable to presidential censure.*

The president personally arranged for Ellen Forbes to meet with the editorial director the following afternoon. During the course of their two-hour discussion, she managed to make at least half a dozen deft references to the issues and questions she and the president had covered the evening before. At the end of the afternoon she was beginning to sound more like an *important presidential emissary* than a young woman seeking employment.

By the time she had arranged her third meeting, with a senior editor engaged in the development of a college political-science textbook program, her persuasive power as a potential employee resided as much in the fact that she enjoyed the confidence and tacit support of the president as it did in her editorial experience. Ellen Forbes was made a job offer during the course of that third meeting largely because she had understood all along that, beyond mere competence, there is an extra political ingredient in most hiring decisions. She staked her claim to employment in this particular instance on the power of the president, a claim that paid off in kind: she was hired. Had she approached the company from any other direction, she probably would have failed. Having only one prospect in her target market, she was able to devote time and trouble to a unique and well-researched approach.

And the emphasis here is on *well-researched.* Operating

at such a high level, the female job hunter simply has to know her stuff. That means slogging through plenty of background material. One woman we spoke to, who cleverly sold her way into the office of a female vice-president of an American-owned, German-based oil company, revealed disconsolately that she threw away a golden opportunity by taking the occasion altogether too lightly. Whiz-bang promotion had afforded her access to a key hiring decision-maker; but superficial interview preparation resulted in her being shown the door after only twenty minutes of discussion. Unlike Ellen Forbes's prospect, this vice-president believed in thoroughly grilling any potential employee who came her way. "The Americans have an expression: 'to fly by the seat of your pants,'" the woman said, smiling grimly. "Well, I tried it that one time and crash-landed."

The bigger the opportunity, the more crucial it is to prepare for it thoroughly. In doing just that, Ellen Forbes was able to achieve two important objectives: win presidential support for her employment initiative, then parlay the politics of that support into persuading those empowered with the ultimate decision of hiring her that *not* offering her a job would be riskier than offering her one. Their president would be more likely to question why his emissary was *not* hired, than why she was.

Presidential power, once borrowed, can only be retrieved by the president himself. So long as he is acquiescent in your use of it, you may do so safely in the knowledge that you will remain largely unopposed in most of the things you try to accomplish in his name. And that includes trying to get hired.

The more that job hunters can successfully persuade high-ranking individuals in the organizations which interest them to participate, however distantly, in their bargaining efforts, the stronger, more plausible those bargaining efforts will be.

Still, aiming high is but one side of the political equation. The other side has to do with convincing those prospects in authority that you are worth supporting in the first place. Winning that support can be as difficult a process as winning the job itself. Ellen Forbes went a long way to solving this problem by the manner in which she promoted her sale: by the way she wrote her introductory letter relating her professional achievements and capacities to her prospect's professional interests and needs, and through the careful presentation of that letter in a polished, compelling, businesslike format.

In Part Three of *The Landau Strategy* we will be telling you much more about the tactics of actual face-to-face negotiations while on the job hunt. But for the moment, at the beginning of the promotion stage of your job hunt, it is enough to understand that promotion *is* negotiation. They are part of the same process and are inspired by the same objective.

Promote your sale as you mean to make it.

6

LANGUAGE

THE TOP-JOB hunt is, promotionally, an exercise in self-advertisement and self-concealment. Language is one of the two major means (packaging is the other) through which you can perform both activities simultaneously, with Machiavellian subtlety.* Language is to the female job hunter what lighting is to the professional photogra-

---

*Niccolò Machiavelli, political scientist and professional sycophant, was by no means as nasty a piece of work as those uninformed about his thought would have us believe.

pher: it adds shading, refinement, diversion. Language can be used to highlight a strength or camouflage a weakness. It can suggest and imply (when you want or need to be evasive), or pinpoint and define (when you want or need to be specific). The bottom line of language is: *it sells*.

While it would be impossible for us, in the course of a single chapter, to convert you into a linguistic wizard (assuming you are not one already), the principles for writing and talking effectively about yourself in a job hunt are not particularly esoteric. They amount to little more than a recognition of your own limitations, an awareness of about eighty key words, and a willingness to follow some simple advice.

We have divided this chapter into two sections. The first, called "Principles and Practices," deals with some of the basic techniques of composing hard-driving prose. We introduce you to a carefully selected group of "buzz-words," verbs we want you to use in your letters and in your résumé. This section concludes with the suggestion, introduced in the previous chapter, that you should relate as much as possible of what you write about yourself to the three yardsticks which efficient organizations have to consider: profit, reward, and growth.

The second section, "Language Persuades," covers the actual composition of your job-hunting communications. We provide you with specimen texts for résumés and letters and, most valuable of all, some practical advice about the use of *copy prefabrication*, the technique of composing promotion material (especially letters) that, though sent to dozens of prospects, appears to have been written with a single, unique prospect in mind.

1. Principles and Practices

In his foreword to a book by John Caples (a vice-president of BBD and O, Inc., a prominent New York advertising agency) called *Tested Advertising Methods*, adman David Ogilvy writes:

> An earlier edition [of this book] taught me most of what I know about writing advertisements.
> For example:

- The key to success lies in perpetual testing of all the variables.
- What you say is more important than how you say it.
- The headline is the most important thing in most advertisements.
- The most effective headlines appeal to the reader's self-interest or give news.
- Long headlines that say something are more effective than short headlines that say nothing.
- Specifics are more believable than generalizations.
- Long copy sells more than short copy.

We have quoted the principles of composition of a celebrated advertising agency entrepreneur (rather than those of an essayist or novelist) because, for the purposes of a job hunt, you are neither an opinion to be expressed nor a character to be developed: you are a product to be promoted. Remember, your résumé is *not* a biography; it is, or ought to be, an advertisement. Understand that and you will understand why so many résumés, which are really misnamed brief biographies, are consigned to the wastebasket by those very people they are intended to persuade.

Except for the first point on Ogilvy's list (on the grounds that testing copy lines is, for an individual job hunter of limited financial resources, unrealistic), every one of the other precepts mentioned is worth adhering to when you start preparing the promotion material for your job search.

Verbs are, as everyone learned in school, "doing words." They convey action, movement, vigor. They suggest, each in its own way, the making of a positive difference. Consider the following list of verbs:*

accelerated	invented	streamlined
accomplished	launched	strengthened
achieved	maintained	stressed
administered	managed	stretched
analyzed	negotiated	structured
approved	organized	succeeded
completed	performed	summarized
conceived	planned	superseded
conducted	processed	supervised
consolidated	produced	terminated
coordinated	programmed	traced
created	projected	tracked
delegated	promoted	traded
delivered	proposed	trained
demonstrated	purchased	transferred
designed	raised profits	trimmed
developed	recommended	tripled/trebled
directed	redesigned	turned
doubled	reduced	uncovered
eliminated	reorganized	unified
established	researched	unraveled
executed	revised	utilized
expanded	revitalized	vacated
generated	scheduled	waged
identified	serviced	widened
implemented	set up	withdrew
improved	simplified	won
increased	sold	worked
initiated	solved	wrote
introduced	started	

*We are grateful to Alan Gregory, of Career Dynamics, Inc., in New York, for permission to reproduce this list.

All these verbs share one feature in common. Without exception they denote that key job-hunting concept: *accomplishment*. Some have the effect of saying, "When I was in a particular job I did this." Others imply, and this is even better, "When I was in a particular job I did this and *that* happened as a result."

If you can show, with respect to either of these propositions, that what you did in your previous or current job either: increased profits (or, the next best thing, saved money); was sufficiently important to generate some kind of personal reward (a raise, a promotion, increased responsibility); or contributed to the growth of the department or division in which you worked, you will be firmly on your way to selling yourself in a manner that properly reflects the realities of business.

2. Language Persuades

You have two devices through which to address those prospects in your target market whom you decide to reach through the mail: the résumé, and the letter. While these items are normally distributed in tandem, it is of course possible (and sometimes even advisable) to incorporate the principal selling features of a résumé into a letter of greater than average length, the so-called résumé/letter.

The Résumé

There are many approaches to résumé writing. Of them all, two work best: the standard, one-page, short-copy approach; and the two- or even three-page, long-copy approach.

Here is an example of the first approach.

RÉSUMÉ A

Name: Caroline Walker

Address: 75 West 84th Street
             Apartment 1201
             New York, N.Y. 10024

             212-724-9110

Education: Master of Arts in Social Psychology, New School for Social Research, June 1968.

             Bachelor of Arts in Psychology, Fairleigh Dickinson University, June 1966.

Employment History

1973–Present: Market Planning and Research Associate, Corporate Staff, Downe Chemicals Ltd.

*Administered** extensive in-house research operation, resulting in total annual savings to the company of more than $250,000.

Initiated major national study relating to changes in corporate image resulting from participation in public service activities.

Participated in the formulation of research designs for new-product exploratory studies.

Established corporate marketing information center.

---

*Buzz words are italicized here for purposes of illustration; they should not be in résumés actually sent out.

Supervised staff of professional and clerical assistants.

1972–1973: Research Project Supervisor, Spitzer, Mills and Bates, Inc.

Implemented all advertising research for major division of automobile manufacturer.

Conducted a major segmentation study of the luxury car market.

Maintained a service relationship with account management and client personnel.

1969–1972: Senior Research Supervisor, Hicks, Sills and David Adv., Inc.

Designed special study on housewives' attitudes toward premiums, published in leading trade journal.

Worked with creative group in translating requests into decision-oriented research.

Worked on major national food and drug brands, including hair-care products and household cleaners.

1967–1969: Project Director, Sloane and O'Brien Adv., Inc.

Supervised research projects for packaged goods and industrial products, including beer, frozen foods, feminine hygiene products, and copying machines.

Special and Professional Qualifications

Who's Who in American Women (1974)

Foremost Women in Communications (1969–1970)

Personal Background

Age: 34

Interests: Theater, Modern Dance, Chess.

This example, which is only a marginally edited version of an existing résumé, works because:

1. It is very simple and specific. It makes no use of any linguistic constructions that are beyond the capability of the average literate person and, with a couple of minor qualifications, has been written within accepted grammatical standards.
2. Accomplishment oriented, it makes heavy and apposite use of the kinds of active verbs we recommend.
3. It builds its appeal around those three bedrock standards of business operation: profit ("Administered extensive in-house research operation resulting in total annual savings to company of more than $250,000"); reward ("Special and Professional Qualifications: *Who's Who in American Women [1974]*"); and growth ("Participated in the formulation of research designs for new-product and exploratory studies").
4. The résumé does not make the mistake of including an abundance of personal detail.

On balance, however, we believe that, provided there is enough relevant material in your job history to justify it, the long-copy approach is the one to adopt. It enables you to present the kind of detail that short-copy simply will not permit. The compression of a four- or five-year employment history onto a single page, especially if during that period you have several substantial accomplishments

to your credit, is quite difficult. So long as they are perti-
nent, credible, and presented without clutter and confu-
sion, those accomplishments make you a most compelling
product for purchase.

Résumé A, though it makes persuasive reading, really
misses as many selling opportunities as it hits—long-copy,
we feel, would have served this woman better. As her résumé stands, it consists of a series of cleverly executed
headlines, largely unsupported by any qualifying text.
If she "established [a] corporate marketing information
center" it would have been useful to know what difference
the creation of such a center made to the quality of marketing information it was intended to distribute, and the
extent to which such information influenced corporate
marketing policy. If she "implemented all advertising
research for [a] major division of [an] automobile manufacturer" it would have been especially interesting to
know to what extent the manufacturer managed to sell
more product as a consequence of those research findings.

The following is a long-copy résumé with a sting in its
tail.

RÉSUMÉ B

Name:	Susan Gonsalves
Address:	118 East 78th Street Apartment 2244 New York, N.Y. 10021
	212-724-8009
Education:	1966–1969 University of Southern Cali- fornia, B.A. History
	1959–1966 San José High School

Employment History

November 1974– | Product Director, International Paints,
Present: | Inc. (New York)

Responsible for one major and three minor corporate brands. *Manage* department of five. Secured position after seventeen months with company as a consequence of two successive promotions from Product Manager to Associate Product Director, then to current assignment.

June 1972– | Product Manager, Standard Brands,
October 1974: | Inc. (Los Angeles)

Supervised one major advertised brand (a shampoo) and *developed* financial and marketing strategy for new product introduction.

September 1969– | Project Supervisor, The Supergroup,
May 1972: | Inc. (Los Angeles)

Hired as market research trainee upon graduation. *Promoted* after three months in-field experience to assistant Project Supervisor. Specialized in fast-moving packaged goods assignments. *Won* promotion to Project Supervisor within nineteen months of joining organization.

Major Accomplishments

Project Director, International Paints, Inc.

Increased *regional sales of major brand-name emulsion paint 210 percent as a result of* introducing *and successfully test-marketing a modified product formulation.*

Initial test-marketing effort indicated sales increases of 52 percent versus control. *Redesigned* packaging, modified promotion strategy, and *strengthened* distribution in light of test-market findings. Product scheduled for major national relaunch.

Created *original incentive program resulting in 73 percent factory sales increase of latex external housepaint during first quarter of 1975.*

Incentive program offered unique discounts on brand-name paintbrushes with proof of product purchase. Test-marketed into metro San Francisco, the program was *expanded* throughout Pacific Northwest.

Designed *financial simulation model for generation of brand profit-and-loss statements.*

Predictive capability of model ranges from five to seven years. Tests price increase sensitivity, provides break-even analyses of incremental marketing expenditures. Adopted corporately, the model has already been modified to conform to seven other brand profiles.

Introduced *consumer self-liquidating offer for 1976 Fall promotion.*

The offer, whose prebooked factory sales results gained 37 percent on corresponding period one year earlier, has since been *expanded* to cover comparable products in other divisions.

Initiated *advertising-concept research on existing print campaign in trade periodicals for brand of enamel paint whose market share had fallen four points in twelve-month period.*

Research findings led to major changes in creative and media strategies resulting:

1. in *stabilizing* brand-market share after precipitous decline
2. in *reducing* media expenditures 12 percent due to increased efficiency of media buy

Product Manager, Standard Brands, Inc.

Conceived, produced *and* tested *three alternative creative executions for TV commercial to support brand in static market-share position.*

The final commercial, placed on-air within two and one half months of initial conception, was instrumental in *raising* brand share 2.0 points in first quarter of 1973 and a further 1.5 points in second quarter.

Identified *$35,000 cost saving in new product research and development project.*

Research analysis suggested refinements in product formulation that would cut development and testing time by 20 percent. *Implemented* further studies whose findings resulted in:

1. a simplified product formulation
2. a 7.5 percent increase in product profitability

Revitalized *market-share position of ailing brand in metro Chicago.*

Developed a creative and media research program to investigate current packaging and promotion strategies supporting brand. *Identified* weaknesses, *wrote* alternative marketing plan, and *implemented* new commercial execution. Reversed previous share decline. Brand subsequently won all-time market share after one year.

Proposed *computer forecast program designed to* strengthen *inventory control.*

System able to accurately forecast unit sales by month, by pack, and by region. Results included:

1. management time savings
2. diminished clerical paperwork
3. speedier product distribution

Project Manager, The Supergroup, Inc.

Sold, *as part of three-person team, a $50,000 research study to major urban newspaper in northern California whose market share was being eroded by competing newspaper.*

Recommended redesign of newspaper format, size, and print. Suggested new price structure for and policy towards the sale and publication of classified ads. Repositioned different categories of news and features according to priorities set by research findings. Results included:

1. circulation gains of 22 percent within one year
2. consequent advertising revenue increase of 34 percent in same period

Executed, *as temporary assistant to Senior Project VP, a $250,000 quantitative and qualitative research study on women—"The New Western Working Woman"—for California affiliate of major New York advertising agency.*

Study *analyzed* West Coast women as consumers, workers, wives, and mothers. *Researched* their demographic and psychographic characteristics, buying tendencies, and banking practices. Conclusions provided agency with authoritative knowledge of West Coast women which:

1. enabled agency to develop more relevant female-oriented ad campaigns
2. *increased* sales of client company products (from perfume to pantyhose) as a result
3. *accelerated* agency account acquisition due to exclusive, specialized knowledge of female consumer

Serviced *the ongoing West Coast research requirements of one of the "Big Three" motor manufacturers.*

Proposed research-derived corporate slogan to meet consumer needs of early seventies. *Recommended* major national study on consumer automotive needs in seventies and eighties in light of economic, energy, and changing social needs.

Special and Professional Qualifications

Bilingual in Portuguese
Working knowledge of French
Member of American Marketing Association

Personal Background

Age: 30

Interests: Backgammon, Bridge, Books

Stylistically, this résumé succeeds particularly well. Like Résumé A, it is accomplishment oriented, and makes scrupulous and compelling use of several hard-hitting active verbs. Almost every headline (those passages appearing in italics) depicts a positive selling proposition. And each proposition is proved by tersely written supporting copy whose appeal is built around profit, reward, and growth.

The evidence contained in this supporting copy is expressed, wherever possible, in either percentage or financial terms. The woman has emphasized all her promotions and has prefaced the résumé with a brief overview of her employment history.

Any potential employer receiving a résumé as compelling as this would be almost derelict in his duty were he not at least to see the applicant. If you have a track record that can be analyzed and described in anything approaching the foregoing terms, you should seriously consider adopting the long-copy résumé.

The Letter

The letter, especially the short-copy, one-page covering letter, is a much misunderstood and misused item in the job hunter's promotional armory. So many job hunters, having composed their résumé, think that a few general lines of text in a covering letter are all they need to write. Their letters have no structure and no logic. They serve no useful purpose because the job hunters responsible for them obviously haven't stopped to consider what possible positive purpose such letters could serve.

The covering letter is more than an appendage to your résumé. Properly written, it can be the promotional lens through which your prospect reads your résumé. More, it can determine whether your prospect bothers to read the résumé at all. Your covering letter should fulfill four vital functions:

- Introduce your résumé.
- Relate the individual elements in the text of your résumé to your prospect's interests and needs.
- Enable you to state concisely (and flexibly) your career objectives.
- Inform your prospect if, and when, and on what terms to expect a follow-up.

Case Study: Jacqueline Casey, Cosmetics Marketing

Jacqueline Casey, since graduating from college with a degree in marketing, had been employed by only two companies. She managed to work her way up from being the secretary to a sales director of the first company, right through to being a marketing manager in the second. During her career she had become competent in a wide variety of areas relating to the marketing of fragrances and cosmetics; from product development and testing, to product introductions and sales forecasting.

For a number of reasons, her chances for continued upward progression with her current employer seemed unlikely, so she decided to look for another job in the same industry. Analyzing her background and experience, she realized that there were basically three categories of potential employers to whom she could apply for a job. In order of importance they were:

A. Fragrance and cosmetics manufacturers, similar to the ones for which she had already worked
B. Advertising agencies with fragrance and cosmetics accounts, who might wish to hire someone with client experience as a means of strengthening their account management capability
C. Market research organizations involved with the fragrance and cosmetics industry

Having isolated these categories of prospects within her target market, she decided to approach thirty-five of them through direct mail. She sent all thirty-five a résumé and a one-page covering letter. Shrewdly, she developed the text of her letter in such a way that she was able to vary the copy in a couple of the middle paragraphs, thus altering the focus and emphasis of her promotion to conform to the differences between the categories of prospects it was designed to reach. Here are the texts of those letters:

LETTER A: To be sent to fragrance and cosmetics manufacturers.

Enclosed you will find a copy of my résumé.

As you will see, I have considerable experience in the fragrance and cosmetics industry, especially in those areas relating to product marketing, product development, and product testing.

I have gained substantial management experience during the past five years and, since joining my present employer in 1973, have been successively promoted through Product and Brand Management to my present position, which is Marketing Manager for a major fragrance division.

Sales oriented, I would ideally like to work in an area offering opportunities for total product marketing, line extensions, and new product development. *

I am available for meetings from March 15 until the end of the month and, needless to say, I would very much like to meet with you during that period to discuss my business background.

---

*Italics are used here to indicate which blocks of copy in each of the subsequent letters have been changed. Do not use italics in letters you are going to send.

LETTER B: To be sent to advertising agencies with fragrance and cosmetics accounts.

Enclosed you will find a copy of my résumé.

As you will see, I have considerable experience in the fragrance and cosmetics industry, especially in those areas relating to product marketing, product development, and product testing.

I have gained substantial management experience during the past five years and, since joining my present employer in 1973, have been successively promoted through Product and Brand Management to my present position, which is Marketing Manager for a major fragrance division.

During the past few years I have been increasingly involved in several important product promotions on behalf of both new and existing product lines, activities that have brought me into close and continuous professional contact with the two major New York advertising agencies handling the products of the division whose marketing effort I manage. That contact has persuaded me that I could make an even greater contribution to the fragrance and cosmetics industry working for an advertising agency than I can now working for a manufacturer.

Sales oriented, I would ideally like to work in an area that offers opportunities for account management and new business acquisition.

I am available for meetings from March 15 until the end of the month and, needless to say, I would very much like to meet with you during that period to discuss my business background.

LETTER C: To be sent to market research agencies.

Enclosed you will find a copy of my résumé.

As you will see, I have considerable experience in the fragrance and cosmetics industry, especially in those areas relating to product marketing, product development, and product testing.

I have gained substantial management experience during the past five years and, since joining my present employer in 1973, have been successively promoted through Product and Brand Management to my present position, which is Marketing Manager for a major fragrance division.

Recently, I have become increasingly interested in and involved with those aspects of market and marketing research that relate to the fragrance and cosmetics industry, from advertising concept testing and D.A.R. analysis of TV commercials, to market segmentation studies and new product testing.

Sales oriented, I would ideally like to work in an area that offers opportunities for account management and new business acquisition.

I am available for meetings from March 15 until the end of the month and, needless to say, I would very much like to meet with you during that period to discuss my business background.

Jacqueline Casey is, in the language of Madison Avenue, "an operator." She *knows.* She put together her job-hunting promotion as if it were an ad campaign for Elizabeth Arden. Her covering letters have zip, flair, and direction. But more than that, they have flexibility.

In each of the three examples, she has modified the copy, depending on the category of prospect she is trying to reach. The variable paragraphs of text can be introduced or withdrawn at will.

"I sent fifteen examples of letter A to primary prospects," Jacqueline Casey explained, "and twelve of letter B to the next most important. I sent letter C to the rest. Since the letters I sent were preprinted, it was no trouble at all to have the lettershop* produce three different versions of what was, basically, a standard text. All I had to do was type in each individual name and address. I saved myself hours of work.''

The principle of copy prefabrication, which can be exploited on a far grander scale than that used by Jacqueline Casey, is routine in many direct mail promotions. It is even possible to apply this principle both to the actual composition of your résumé/letter and to your résumé, varying their textual emphasis to conform to the categories of prospects within your target market.

The Résumé/Letter

An alternative approach to a letter accompanied by a résumé is the long-copy, two- or three-page résumé/letter. This incorporates a summary of the details of a résumé within the more personal format of a letter.

The following example was sent to a variety of prospects with senior management responsibilities in the marketing divisions of approximately eighty of the largest corporations based in New York. We have chosen this letter because it demonstrates how a young woman, without a particularly extensive employment history, was able to make herself appear dynamic, highly motivated, and very successful. Again, this résumé/letter is built around those three vital business principles: profit, reward, and growth. It works.

> I am looking for a position as a marketing executive with an organization, like your own, that will utilize, appreciate, and reward my strengths. I am a sales personality, with an ability to comprehend and cope with reams of technical data and other paperwork, and a penchant for long hours.

---

*An offset printing concern specializing in small-scale printing and graphic design projects; discussed in detail in the next chapter.

Upon graduating from college (Hofstra University, cum laude, December 1973, Sociology) I took a secretarial position with my current employer, The International Response Group, one of the largest direct marketing organizations in the world, because I saw an opportunity for a professional career. Now, four years later, I've outgrown them.

Within my first ten months of employment, I was promoted to an executive-level position as Assistant Business List Manager in charge of servicing clients who rented our mail-order business lists.

In 1975 my immediate superior was transferred to our Los Angeles office, and I was promoted to Manager—the first woman ever to hold this position in the New York office. In 1975 and 1976 I was the highest billing account executive in I.R.G.'s Business List Department, nationwide.

In June 1976 I was promoted out of the Business List Department to full-fledged Account Executive servicing our consumer direct mail clients with a complete range of services: lists, research, printing and production, computer work, creative work, etc. By the end of 1977, I had achieved the highest billings of any Account Executive in our New York branch. At present, I am fully responsible for servicing two of our largest and most sensitive clients.

My experience includes both new business presentation and client contact on the highest level of management. And because I came up "through the ranks," I have an ingrained understanding of backroom procedures and the pesky details of implementing major projects. I believe that this combination of talents is unusual and valuable.

I look forward to hearing from you.

The secret of the success of this résumé/letter has to do with the fact that every paragraph represents an achievement-oriented selling proposition on behalf of the individual it describes. Each proposition grabs the reader's attention and draws that attention on down through the text to the next paragraph, and the next.

The letter is immediate, somewhat personal, and, seemingly, written from the heart. And, of course, its short, sharp paragraphing is particularly suitable for copy prefabrication.

Except in those instances when your résumé is distributed by a headhunter, it is up to you to control the manner in which your résumé and covering letter, or résumé/letter, is presented to your prospect.

Just as the importance of the letter accompanying a résumé is frequently overlooked by the job hunter, so too is the vehicle in which the job hunter's promotional material is delivered—the envelope. In order that it reach your prospect unopened, mark your envelope *Personal*, or *Private and Confidential*, in the lower right-hand corner. It will then become a part of the mail that he opens first and with particular attention. Also, be sure your name and address appear in the upper left-hand corner.

Part Three of *The Landau Strategy* contains several other suggestions and tips for the effective use of language in your job hunt. As must be clear to many of you, the capacity to use language convincingly comes easily to comparatively few. An increasingly audio-visual environment has provoked a much-criticized crisis of literacy in our society. Even at senior levels of business, the ability to write and speak well is rare. Yet business people generally respond very favorably to *written* communications that are executed with concision and clarity, conviction and finesse.

If there is a secret to linguistic success on your job hunt it is, perhaps, no more than this: recognize your limitations and adapt the compositional advice we have offered to suit your own professional interests and needs. And *think* short: short paragraphs, short sentences, short words.

7

PACKAGING

PACKAGING IS THE art of
the raised expectation. It is
making something look better than it really is. Handled
shrewdly, even the most flimsy employment history can
be made to seem exciting and significant. And the least
prepossessing candidate, for the investment of a few dollars, can be made to appear vigorous and original. There is
absolutely nothing dishonest about making yourself *look*
terrific, either on paper or in the flesh. On the contrary, the
trouble you have taken to present yourself in the best
possible light constitutes both a compliment to your prospective employer (you are taking that opportunity se-

riously) and a statement about yourself (you are willing and able to produce stylish, meticulous work).

Divided into two sections, this chapter deals with a pair of separate but related issues: how the female job hunter should appear on paper ("Packaging Your Past") and how she should appear in person ("Packaging Your Personality"). The chapter is underpinned by what might appear to be an unlikely idea: *restraint*. Of all the stratagems you adopt in your job hunt, those connected with packaging ought to be the most reserved, the least likely to offend. The way you package yourself is a refinement, a visual nuance. At the promotion stage of a job hunt, the package *is* the product. Which is all the more reason for you to avoid packaging theatrics. The baroque is out. Think cool, clean, classic.

1. Packaging Your Past

Package your past accomplishments to influence the way your prospects see you. Develop your package so that it enables your prospects to picture how you might fit into their organization. Bankers are, as a general rule, case studies in rectitude: firm of jaw, stern of eye, dry of handshake. Remember that, when you package your past for them. Admen are more accessible, less rigid—or so most of them would have us believe. They think of themselves as witty, suave. Remember that, too.

Package yourself as your prospects package *themselves*.

The last chapter told you how to analyze and then describe your background and accomplishments in language. This one tells you how to take that language and present it in a visual style that is clear, coherent, and compelling. Here, you will find specimen layouts for each of the three alternative approaches to résumé composition we described in the previous chapter: the short-copy, single-page résumé; the long-copy résumé; and the résumé/letter. There are specimen layouts for a covering letter and an envelope, as well.

Our visual approach is built around the idea of graphic continuity. This means that, whatever linguistic formula you decide to adopt, the three elements (only two if you go with the résumé/letter format) of the final package will have a shared visual character: headlines and body copy will be consistent; typefaces and paper stock will match. Our objective is this: to help you prepare a total promotion package written and designed in a manner that conveys a sense of your uniqueness as a businesswoman.

The kind of visual style we recommend is, unfortunately, unobtainable without the use of professional help. This is perhaps the only time in your job hunt when you will need the advice and direct assistance of an outside resource. But, if you are really going to put some visual zip into your promotion, professional advice is what you need. Such advice is rarely cheap. However, knowing exactly what you want can minimize the costs considerably.

Your best move is to discuss the entire project with your local lettershop. If you are not sure where one is, consult the Yellow Pages under the category entitled "Printers." There, you will find all kinds of entries for small concerns that specialize in offset printing, letterheads, duplicating, and photocopying. Any one of these firms can almost always offer graphic design services for a reasonable fee. You should be able to negotiate a total price for the entire assignment: paper, envelopes, graphic design, typesetting, printing. All you have to do is provide the text for your résumé and letters.

The following layouts represent no more than visual guidelines. They will give you an idea of what the finished version of each element in your promotion package might look like when it is finally printed. The layouts will also enable you to clearly present your requirements to the printer that you select to produce the finished promotion material.

In each layout we have suggested typefaces and paper stock. These are intended to be guides, not definitive recommendations. Your printer will help you select the paper and type style that you find most attractive and most appropriate to the field in which you seek employment. Be prudent. Be subtle. Be austere. You are trying to win that top job, not land a six-week nightclub engagement in Vegas.

The Short-Copy Résumé

Consider the design features of this layout (corresponding to the text of Résumé A). Its visual logic is impeccable: headlines match, body copy runs comfortably down through the page. The emphasis throughout is on clarity, concision. This résumé tells your prospect that you are organized, fastidious, and to the point.

THE SHORT-COPY RÉSUMÉ

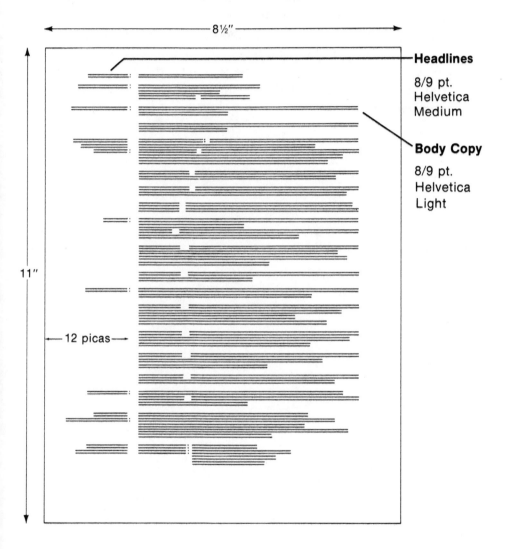

The Long-Copy Résumé

Designed to cover three pages, this layout (corresponding to the text of Résumé B) has been put together in the form of a brochure or small booklet. The outside page carries your name and address; the inside pages and, if necessary, the outside back page, carry the text. Again, the visual character of this résumé is one of refinement and restraint.

Résumé

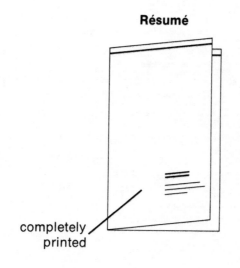

completely
printed

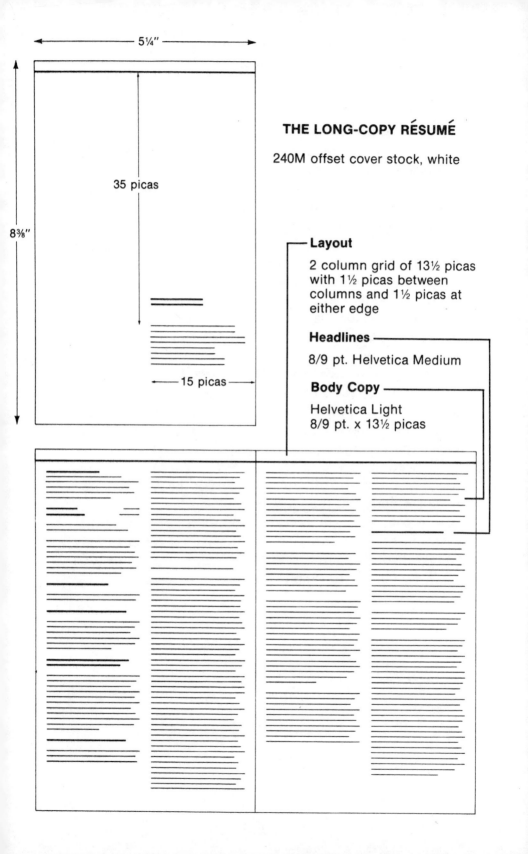

THE LONG-COPY RÉSUMÉ

240M offset cover stock, white

Layout

2 column grid of 13½ picas
with 1½ picas between
columns and 1½ picas at
either edge

Headlines

8/9 pt. Helvetica Medium

Body Copy

Helvetica Light
8/9 pt. x 13½ picas

5¼"

8⅜"

35 picas

15 picas

The Résumé/Letter

Since this is intended to be a personal communication (corresponding to the text of the Résumé/Letter), it is clearly inappropriate to have the text typeset. Using a good carbon ribbon in your typewriter (which will make anything you produce look particularly sharp), type the text of the letter on plain bond paper and, depending on how many such letters you intend to mail, have the letter-shop offset print them onto your letterhead (which that same lettershop will print for you). Note that the typeface recommended for the letterhead corresponds to that recommended for your résumé and for the return address on your envelopes.

Then all you have to do is type in the individual names, titles, and addresses of your prospects (using, needless to say, the same typewriter as you used to type the original), and you will have created letters that appear to be completely personalized.

If necessary, you may decide to print two or three (maybe even more) different versions of the résumé/letter, to correspond to the different categories of prospects within your target market that you wish to reach. In that event, just type the alternate versions of the letter (it may simply involve modifications to only a paragraph or two) and have your lettershop print them in batches.

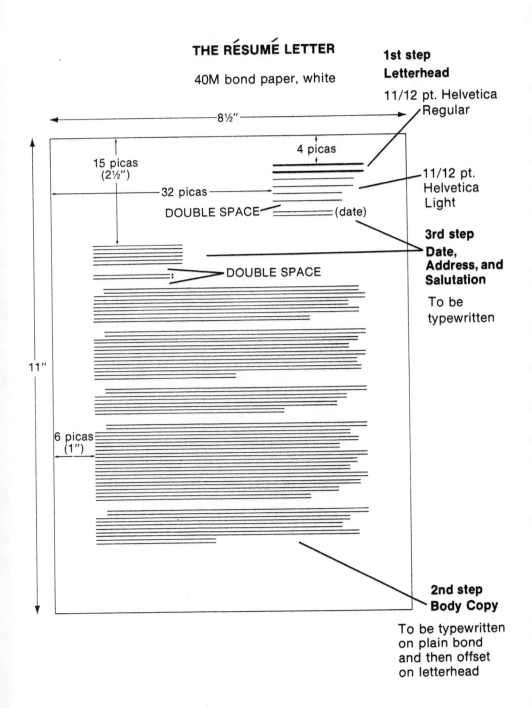

THE RÉSUMÉ LETTER

40M bond paper, white

1st step
Letterhead

11/12 pt. Helvetica Regular

8½"

4 picas

15 picas
(2½")

32 picas

11/12 pt. Helvetica Light

DOUBLE SPACE — (date)

3rd step
Date, Address, and Salutation

To be typewritten

DOUBLE SPACE

11"

6 picas
(1")

2nd step
Body Copy

To be typewritten on plain bond and then offset on letterhead

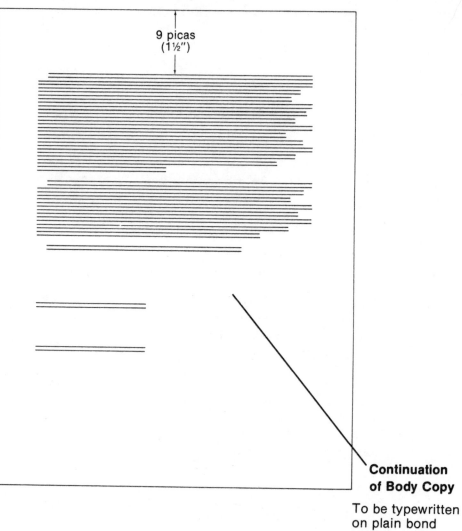

9 picas
(1½")

**Continuation
of Body Copy**

To be typewritten
on plain bond
and then offset
on letterhead

The Résumé Letter (*continued*)

The Covering Letter

Although the letterhead will be printed, it is not our suggestion that you actually have the text of your covering letters typeset. On the contrary, they must look as original as possible. Use the technique outlined in the earlier section dealing with the production of a résumé/letter; type the text(s) of your covering letter and have the lettershop offset them in the quantities you require.

THE COVERING LETTER

40M bond paper, white

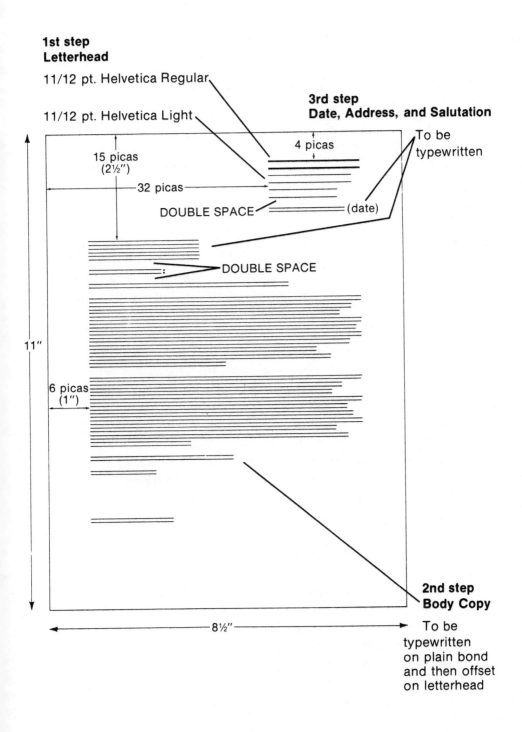

**1st step
Letterhead**

11/12 pt. Helvetica Regular

11/12 pt. Helvetica Light

**3rd step
Date, Address, and Salutation**

To be typewritten

4 picas

15 picas
(2½")

32 picas

DOUBLE SPACE

(date)

DOUBLE SPACE

11"

6 picas
(1")

**2nd step
Body Copy**

To be typewritten on plain bond and then offset on letterhead

8½"

The Envelope

If you want the visual character of your envelope to correspond to the visual character of the other elements in your promotion package, you will have to consider first, whether the envelope is available in the shade of paper stock you are planning to use for your résumé and letter; and second, whether or not you feel it is necessary to print your name and return address on your envelopes.

This second consideration is optional. While having the lettershop print your name and address on the envelope (remember to use the same typeface as you use for your letterhead and résumé) adds an extra element of pizazz, it may constitute an unjustifiable added expense. However, if you do decide that it will make a difference, position your name and address either on the flap or on the upper left-hand corner of the envelope's face.

Then all you have to do is type in the name, title, and address of your prospect, taking care to add the key injunction "Private and Confidential" in the lower right-hand corner of the envelope.

Like most aspects of your job hunt, the secret to the successful production of your promotion material is planning and preparation. Decide, ahead of time, what you want to achieve in terms of the visual appeal of your promotion, get good technical advice, and leave it to the lettershop to execute. The assignment you have given them is no different from assignments they receive from commercial organizations every day.

Just remember this: packaging is intended to enhance, not detract from, what you write about yourself in your letters and in your résumé. It tells your prospects that you are different, that you are prepared to go to special lengths to get what you want, that you are unafraid of the fresh approach, that you are capable of going that additional, difficult yard. Packaging your past says: "I am a deadly serious candidate."

THE ENVELOPE

No. 2 catalogue envelope, white

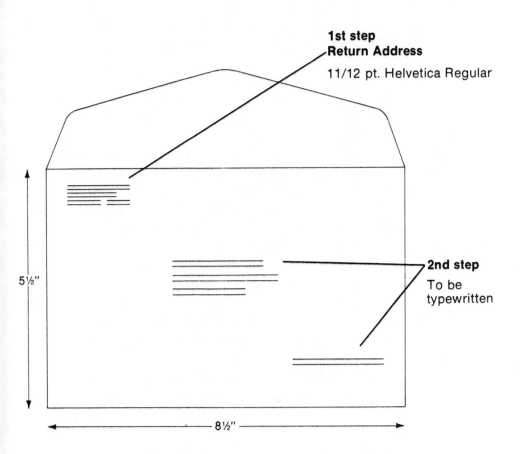

1st step
Return Address

11/12 pt. Helvetica Regular

2nd step

To be
typewritten

5½"

8½"

2. Packaging Your Personality

Dress as if you mean business. Dress for the business in which you mean to work. The straighter the industry, the straighter you must look. Imitation is the sincerest form of flattery, so it makes sense to dress as those to whom you are selling yourself dress. And if you don't know how they dress, spy on them.

Suppose, for example, you want to work for a trust company. Spend a few minutes of your lunch hour outside the offices of the biggest one you can find. Observe how the women who work there package themselves. Look at their hair, their shoes, their dresses. Compare and contrast those who look like account executives with those who look like secretaries. Dress like those who look like account executives. If you think you would feel more comfortable dressing like those who appear to be secretaries, you shouldn't be reading this book.

Dress comfortably. Interviewers will sense if the outfit you are wearing has been bought brand-new for the occasion (not necessarily a bad thing) and is one to which you are unaccustomed. Choose styles that not only suit you but that also conform to the context in which you are selling yourself.

Stay away from bright, extreme colors. Reds and yellows are out except, of course, when used tactically to throw into relief an otherwise muted total effect. A scarlet breast-pocket kerchief (you are capable of an occasional flash of brilliance, right?) can work well if you have the confidence to carry it off.

Go first class. All the elements of your total look should be as fine as you can make them. The fabrics and textures you wear say as much about you as the way you speak and act. The difference in effect between wool, silk, or gabardine (fabrics that tell of your taste and individuality) and nylon, plastic, and most other synthetics (fabrics that speak of cheapness and unoriginality) can, in an important job interview, be profound.

Clothes

Irrespective of the business they were in, most executives we interviewed (male and female) said that the fail-safe clothing formula for a business meeting is a well-tailored skirt suit and a fine blouse. The suit should be smart, discreet, and inoffensive.

Variations of the tailored suit work well, too. Consider a tailored skirt, a shirt, and a blazer. The advantage of this outfit is that the elements are interchangeable and can be made to appear more or less formal according to the occasion. *Two skirts, four blouses, and one blazer can enable you to produce a number of different looks and styles.*

Other suitable outfits are dresses with jackets. However, business dresses are more difficult to select—unless you are careful, they can make you appear overfeminine. Steer clear of the voiles, the frills, and the flounces if you attend your meetings in a dress.

Accessories

Accessories should live up to their name, that is, they should complement and enhance, rather than detract from, your total look. They must reflect discretion, subtlety. In an interview, you should come across as a serious-minded businesswoman, not a femme fatale.

Shoes

Certain senior executives, like many headwaiters, have the knack of identifying a person's essential quality by the way they are shod. Charles Revson, we were told, judged his subordinates by the quality of their footwear. Apocryphal or not, this story suggests that shoes are, in one sense, like underwear: the more expensive they are, the classier you feel. And look.

Make sure your shoes are of good plain leather, moderate in design (fancy buckles and other snappy, unusual refinements are to be avoided), and comfortable. Especially the latter. It is not unusual for potential employers to suggest, especially if you have performed convincingly in the interview, that they show you around. Be prepared for that possibility by wearing shoes you can confidently walk in. And stick to muted colors: black, navy, brown, maroon.

Handbag/Briefcase

Business meetings involve plenty of handshaking, so try to keep at least one hand free. That means you are in an either/or situation when it comes to carrying a handbag or a briefcase. In general, the trend among businesswomen these days is to eliminate a handbag entirely and to carry makeup materials, keys, etc., in their briefcase.

Your briefcase should be simple and businesslike. Black or brown leather is preferable, although there are some particularly expensive models available for women in suede and Ultrasuede. If you don't own one, you may find it cheaper to borrow one from a friend. In any event, try to find a briefcase sufficiently spacious to accommodate a small, collapsible umbrella.

Clearly, there are situations (like a lunch meeting, for example) when a briefcase is unnecessary and even inappropriate. So if you decide you need a handbag, it should be on the small side. Don't carry anything too cumbersome or fancy. And don't carry a handbag with which you are ill at ease, one that obliges you to constantly reposition it; from shoulder to lap to hand to underarm. Such acrobatics will make you appear nervous.

Gloves

Except in midsummer, carry gloves, even if you don't wear them. Provided that they complement your outfit, they add an extra dimension of professionalism and flair to any woman's appearance.

Jewelry
Cut jewelry to a minimum. Avoid things that jangle and glitter. A few good, discreet items of jewelry do more for you than several loud pieces.

Makeup
It is impossible to tell you what kind of makeup you should wear. A general rule, though, is not to go to extremes. If you wear absolutely no makeup, it may imply to the interviewer that you don't care about your appearance and that if you neglect yourself, you may also neglect certain aspects of your work. On the other hand, a heavily made-up face can suggest a nature given to overinvolvement with itself. How can a woman so absorbed in herself devote the right amount of attention to her job?

And it's important to recognize, as well, the sexual connotations associated with heavy makeup. A male interviewer will, consciously or unconsciously, take note and respond accordingly. Then, no matter how professional your performance, no matter how polished your pitch, part of your businessperson image will be spoiled.

If you are not sure about your makeup, or if you want a new look for interviews, women's magazines are full of advice on cosmetics, and they always give detailed and precise information about brands and their availability. Department stores offer opportunities for you to walk around the various counters and look at the women who work there. Many cosmetics firms train their own sales forces, especially those who represent them in major stores. Which group of representatives do you want to look like when you go for your major interviews? Ask them for help and advice and tell them why. Be careful, though— saleswomen are there to sell, so don't, unless you really feel that you need them, buy dozens of items that you may never use.

Department stores also regularly stage promotions for cosmetics houses with a makeup artist invariably on hand. Let her redo your face, once you have explained your special needs. But again, don't get trapped into buying all the creams and lotions that are on display.

As for your hands, the keynote is neatness. If you wear nail polish, it must be properly applied, not chipped or cracked. And your nails should all be the same length, more or less. Probably, the "safest" hands have medium-length nails, neatly manicured and covered with a clear or inoffensive neutral polish—or no nail polish at all. Many people we spoke to said they hated to see interviewees with long red talons, because a sexual rather than a businesslike attitude was projected. Also, like the overly made-up face, such nails imply self-absorption and a reluctance to become involved; certainly they hinder physical involvement in some activities.

The issue of perfume also came up during our talks with women. It was generally agreed that wearing a fragrance to an interview is entirely appropriate as long as it's light rather than heavy, and an eau de toilette rather than a perfume. Wear enough to make you feel good, but if your prospect asks you what brand of perfume you have on, he's been sidetracked by your smell—it's too obtrusive. One person we spoke to mentioned that she once interviewed a young woman who wore so much sweet, sickly, offensive perfume that it made her head spin. She got that young woman out of her office in about ten minutes and had to leave her door wide open for the rest of the day to get rid of the odor.

Hair

Length of hair, in itself, is unimportant—it's what you do with it that counts. The keynote, again, is neatness. Be well groomed.

If your hair is short, get a good, simple haircut. Don't wear a hairstyle that covers half your face or necessitates your constantly pushing the hair out of your eyes. Businessmen don't bother with their hair; you shouldn't either.

If your hair is long, don't wear it loose. Keep in mind that, in the interview situation, the prospect is actually seeing the product package. And that product is a businesswoman, not a cover girl. The image you project when you wear your long hair loose is drastically different from the one you project if your long hair is pulled back into a chignon. By walking into a male prospect's office with long, bewitching hair you run the risk of wiping out a lot of good work achieved by your promotion package. Like heavy makeup, long hair has sexual overtones.

A word on "afros." Get them trimmed. Women have been known not to get job offers, despite brilliant qualifications, because their potential bosses were turned off by "afros out to there."

———

Don't be tyrannized by the suggestions we have made in this chapter. Modify as needed those that suit your instincts and tastes; discard the rest. Our only dogmatic recommendation is that you remember: appearances count. When Oscar Wilde said that "a well-tied tie is the first serious step in life," he was making a sociological, as well as a sartorial, observation.

8

THE LAUNCH

O VER-ORCHESTRATION
is the archenemy of the pains-
takingly planned, creatively designed job hunt. A function of fear, not perfectionism, over-orchestration is the
last refuge of the unself-confident promoter. Its symptom
is the moist palm. Its antidote is action. A launch, remember, is a launch: a cutting loose and a letting go. Don't
hesitate. Jump.

Be hard-nosed. Let your prospects know who you are
and what you want. Fuel the mails, pepper your referrals
with polite, forthright requests for help, ingratiate yourself with headhunters, and hit the phone. A promotion is a

juggling act: all the disparate elements of the effort have, in a relatively short time, to be drawn together, assembled, organized, and then directed accurately towards an unsuspecting, and therefore undefended, target market.

Attack. The launch stage of a promotion can rarely be executed in a day. Depending on the scale of your effort and the amount of time you have available to put it into effect, it could take three or four. But the smart promoter knows better than to let that launch drag on for weeks. Snap it out quickly. It's more efficient. And it will give you a super psychological boost.

We talked to dozens of women who complained about how time-consuming and hence irritating their job hunts became. But we discovered that all too often their annoyance stemmed from a simple failure to execute each stage of their campaign decisively and quickly.

One woman declared that getting her résumés into the mail "just went on and on for days." She grumbled about spending most of her evenings for an entire week "licking envelopes." On further examination it turned out that she never really sat down for a few hours' sustained effort to get the job out of the way; rather, she dallied over what is an admittedly boring task by breaking up the monotony with phone calls to friends, sessions in front of the TV, interruptions to wash her hair, time-outs for an overdue manicure.

Now this is just plain dumb.

Tough out the tedium by putting Beethoven on your stereo (the Fifth and the *Eroica* symphonies have the kind of inspirational quality you'll find appropriate to your ambitions), pour yourself an eight-ounce glass of white wine, and stick to it until the job's done.

Unless you are very fortunate, responses to your launch will not start filtering through for five or six days after you have made your initial contacts (except, of course, for those contacts made by telephone). Stay loose. Relax. Play some tennis, jog, visit friends. Let the momentum build. The last thing you should do is worry about whether or not your effort is going to produce the positive consequences your early planning entitles you to expect. It will.

Two tactical tips about timing and response analysis: don't underrate the value of either in your job-hunting campaign. An ill-timed launch, like an ill-timed joke, reflects adversely on the individual responsible for it. The same is true of a crudely analyzed (or, worse, unanalyzed) promotion. Analysis is the job hunter's public opinion poll; it can be an external and objective check of how well (or badly) your public perceives you. Learn from it.

1. Timing

A mistimed launch will depress your response rates considerably. Various industries, you should remember, go through periods of the year when they are particularly busy and when their senior personnel are consequently less likely to be accessible to an employment approach. The cosmetics and fragrance business is especially preoccupied in February and June, as it prepares for its spring and fall promotions. Book publishers are reputed to be intensely busy in September and October, tying up the details of projects designed to reach the market in the spring of the following year.

It will be very much to your advantage as well to try to discover the extent to which seasonal factors influence the rate of resignations in the industry you are planning to join, because those resignations represent additional employment opportunities for you. In general, people are less inclined to make career moves during the last month of any year for fear of prejudicing year-end bonuses. Once Christmas bonuses have been paid, however, corporate loyalty diminishes and, in the new year, people who are looking for new jobs do so with special enthusiasm. And so should you if you want to fill one of those vacancies.

The following table (which resulted from a three-year test program for a nonseasonal item) is regularly referred to by direct marketers as proof of the seasonality of responses to their promotions. The figures are given in percentages.

The most responsive month is rated 100 percent.

January	100.0	July	73.3
February	96.3	August	87.0
March	71.0	September	79.0
April	71.5	October	89.9
May	71.5	November	81.0
June	67.0	December	79.0

Significantly, a number of recruitment consultants with whom we spoke acknowledged that there were important parallels between this table and their own experience of fluctuations in the job market. The summer months, especially June and July, tend to be unfavorable ones both for promoting mail-order merchandise and for changing jobs. The late summer and early fall period is one where many people seem disposed to change employers, though the best possible time appears to be the new year. Needless to say, your launch will be most advantageously set in motion during a highly responsive month.

In addition to making a seasonal adjustment to the timing of the launch stage of your campaign, you should also consider, particularly if you plan a heavy direct mail effort, at what time of the week to reach your prospect. Avoid Monday morning's deluge of mail. Postal services being what they are, you can be fairly sure that mail delivered in bulk on Saturday will probably arrive at its destination the following Tuesday or Wednesday.

While you can do nothing to control the timing of approaches made on your behalf by active referrals or headhunters, you can control your own telephone approaches. Between 8:45 and 9:30 A.M. is usually the best time to reach prospects by telephone. They tend to be fresher and more receptive then; they've just had their coffee, but their meetings have yet to start. And in reaching them early in their business day, you are relaying an important message: "I'm on the ball," you are telling them, "and ready to run with it."

2. Response Analysis

Smart promoters keep a thumb and forefinger on the public pulse. They look for, and react to, minute changes in the collective attitude of their market. They capitalize on opportunities, circumvent setbacks. Shrewd diagnosticians, they supplement their own best instincts with statistics. Numbers, they know, count. Make them count for you.

You will remember that we discussed (in "Media") the necessity for not putting all your promotional eggs in one basket. By that we were referring to the care you should take to ensure that your promotion is properly distributed through the four media devices (direct mail, referrals, headhunters, the telephone) you have at your disposal through which to reach your target market. As a means of making that distribution process easier, and to facilitate an accurate analysis of response, we have put together a *Campaign Execution Schedule.*

Consider the following simple example.

Suppose that there are 100 prospects in your target market (we expect that many of you will develop a more extensive universe of prospects than this) and that you have divided them into three categories: primary (the most important), secondary (less important), and tertiary (the least important). For the sake of the example, assume that you have identified 25 examples of the first, 50 of the second, and 25 of the third. If you follow our advice, you will try to reach those prospects through each of the four media alternatives. In our example we have tended to favor direct mail over referrals and headhunters. You may decide to make the distribution more even or, depending on your own understanding of your target market, to favor another of the four media options at the expense of the remaining three.

As you can see from the following table, we have decided to reach 10 of our primary prospects through direct mail, 8 through active referrals, 4 through passive referrals, 2 by means of headhunters, and only 1 via the telephone. Moving cumulatively across the three columns of prospects, you will see that, out of our original 100, 70 are destined to be reached by direct mail, 15 through referrals, 9 through headhunters, and 6 via the telephone.

The second part of the Campaign Execution Schedule

Campaign Execution Schedule

Campaign Execution Schedule		Target Market			
		Primary Prospects	Secondary Prospects	Tertiary Prospects	Total Prospects Within Target Market
		25	50	25	100
Direct Mail	Shotgun	—	35	20	[55]
					70
	Rifle	10	5	—	[15]
Media Options Referrals	Active	8	—	—	[8]
					15
	Passive	4	3	—	[7]
Headhunters		2	4	3	[9]
The Telephone		1	3	2	[6]

deals with response analysis. With respect to each media option, we have divided your possible responses into four categories. They range in intensity from the most positive ("Formal Interview Granted") to the least responsive ("Nothing Doing"). The last two columns ("Cumulative Positive Response" and "Cumulative Percentage Response") are the key to the statistical analysis of your entire promotion.

According to the hypothetical responses we have filled in, the most responsive media option proves to be passive referrals (50 percent), followed by direct mail (33 percent). The remaining options are working significantly less well. The lesson here is obvious. Promotions are about patterns. They deal, at least as far as their consequences are concerned, in the workable and the unworkable. Patterns tell you about which of your media options are most, and least, responsive. Learn to be ruthless in your management of them. Support those that succeed; eliminate those that fail.

Sentimentality has no place in the job hunt. The deeper you are drawn into the rhythm of your campaign,

Response Analysis						
Formal Interview Granted	You Sound Interesting	Let's Just Talk	See Personnel	Nothing Doing	Cumulative Positive Response	Cumulative Percentage Response
—	1	2	1	5	3	5%
2	2	1	—	10	5	33%
1	—	1	1	5	3	27%
1	1	1	1	3	4	50%
1	—	—	—	8	1	10%
—	—	1	—	5	1	17%

the less tolerant you will become of the promotional devices that fail you. You will, imperceptibly perhaps, toughen. Especially towards yourself. And that is just as well. Exhaustively planned and impeccably promoted though your sale has been so far, *making* that sale is harder still.

Top jobs are won and lost in the cold context of face-to-face confrontation. Here is where the hardest sell begins.

PART THREE

MAKING YOUR SALE

9

THE SECRET OF SELLING

MAKING YOUR SALE is a grueling, exhilarating physical and mental experience. It will stretch you to the limit. Suitable neither for the weak of mind nor the weak of will, this third and final stage of your job-hunting campaign represents a massive, sustained exercise in human relations. During it you will encounter a dozen different personality types: fast-talkers, low-key smoothies, gutless incompetents, manic entrepreneurs, outright bores.

You will have to become adept at handling (and winning over) everyone from the young, pin-striped hustler to the fashionable superwoman who has kicked and scratched her way to the top and means to stay there. The interest of such people in you is limited precisely to how you can help *them*.

Fortunately, modern business is not run entirely by amoral corporate climbers. From time to time you will be charmed and excited to meet intelligent, decent people of both sexes and all ages who will impress you with their composure, self-confidence, aggressiveness, and humor. Sure of their talent and comfortable with their success, such people will invariably be solicitous and helpful. Honest though their efforts to assist you may be, never be lulled into complacency. Keep thinking. Stay on your toes. Remember, you are being *watched*.

This last phase in your campaign is harder than the first two because, suddenly, you have nothing to hide behind. You've gone public. Your successes and shortcomings are on display. A copywriting error could be erased and revised; a miscalculated percentage play could be analyzed and adjusted; an improvident media decision could be caught and corrected; an ineffective layout could be redesigned; a poorly executed printing job returned. Now, other than how you dress, you have neither camouflage nor cover. False moves are irreversible. At and beyond the vice-presidential corporate level, everything you do will be scrutinized with the utmost care—right down to how you carry a briefcase, enter a room, shake a hand, cross your legs.

There are no second chances in a top-job interview.

That nervous, tentative period is over. Return mail has started to build: two letters on the fifth day, six on the seventh, eleven on the tenth. A headhunter calls to announce that "things look positive." (This means that he's interested the person presently employed in the job he thinks would interest you, in a position elsewhere—after, of course, having interested whoever is occupying *that* position in a third job. Not for nothing are headhunters called headhunters!) Other calls come in. Telephone calls are good news. They mean you've turned people on. More, they suggest immediate opportunities. The promo's beginning to bite. One prospect in ten wants to see you about "upcoming openings." Two in fifteen want to "explore possibilities." The odd prospect in twenty-five tells you there are no jobs, but congratulates you on the graphic and linguistic verve of your résumé, and suggests you get together anyway. Take that one seriously, especially if the signature's above a fancy title—anything presidential or vice-presidential, pursue. Respond to anything from "personnel" with extreme caution.

Relax. Keep cool. Have the clothes you intend to wear to interviews cleaned and pressed. Remember who's in control. Stay on top of your promotion. Analyze your current responses in light of the original categories of prospects you established at the planning stage of your job hunt. Select at least four positive responses from organizations in which you are the least interested, and go see them first. The gravest error you can make now is to initiate negotiations with one of your hottest prospects *too early*. The name of the game, even though your market is opening up nicely, is still "testing." Get your interview style in shape with a few quiet nonessential meetings. Everyone blows at least one major pitch in a job hunt, but at least you can minimize the risks.

Stand pat during your first few interviews. Let the prospects do the work. Ask questions. Don't talk too much. Try to get a feel for how the prospect responds to you: engagingly? with deliberate reserve? suspiciously? Make notes afterwards about the kinds of questions you were asked and in what sequence. Don't even attempt to seriously sell yourself. This is a rehearsal, a good-natured reading of the script. As time goes by there will be revisions, changes. See if you can make your prospect want to buy you. If your impression after thirty minutes of discussion is that he does, congratulate yourself. It's a terrific indicator of your likely future success.

Keep testing. In your first few meetings try shading several of your past accomplishments: emphasize some at the expense of others. Then try it the other way around.

After a number of these encounters, you'll be in a strong position to assess what parts of your background and experience "play" and what parts don't. Soon, you'll begin to notice various kinds of response patterns in your interviews, and those patterns will be repeated again and again. As your experience in interviews grows, you'll come to recognize the location of major minefields. You'll know to stay away from politics, personalities, and religion— that fiendish-looking, hip-sounding, cynical hustler may turn out to be a Christian Scientist. Only name-drop if you're *very* confident. It's a small world. The person you know and love might be the same person who did your prospect out of a fifty-thousand-dollar deal the day before.

Take a look at the numbers again. The chapter on "Playing the Percentages" warned you that, however sensational you contrived to look on paper, your response rate would be only a modest fraction of the total number of prospects in your target market at best. Are you on target? If your original projections are being met, relax. If not, maybe you need to fuel the mails again with another fifty promotion packages. Keep that bottom line (an acceptable ratio of offers to interviews) in super shape: the success of your campaign (and your own self-confidence) depends on it.

Now is the time to start moving confidently, decisively. You've paid your dues to logistics, to planning. You've psyched yourself up with some easy-paced early meetings. You handled them comfortably. You can feel your authority building. You are almost ready for the deadly serious business of selling.

Selling is a subtle activity, one involving a series of cleverly calculated stylistic shifts and nuances. It has its own inner pace and tempo. Those most accomplished at selling are successful at three things: listening, watching, and adapting.

No two selling situations are exactly alike. Every sale is original and unique.

There are, however, certain selling formulas that provide a variety of stylistic structures upon which your presentations can be built. There are, we think, four of them. (Actually there are five. But no one in her right mind would try to *undersell* an employment prospect. That would be dumb. Very dumb.)

1. The hard sell
2. The soft sell
3. The oversell
4. Hard selling with a soft-sell style

Except for the fourth, these selling styles are well known to people professionally engaged in selling. They are as much a part of the vocabulary of selling as are certain tactical plays in professional football.

Clearly, each style implies a very different approach to selling. That approach is determined by a single, unalterable reality: the prospect. An informal rule of thumb suggesting the selling style to adopt is this: the tougher, more skeptical the interrogation, the more aggressive and forthright your selling approach should be.

The following tactical summaries are intended to be no more than irreverent, impressionistic guidelines. Only you can decide which selling style to adopt and under what circumstances it can most effectively be used. Accomplished salespeople are adept at combination selling: hard sell drifting into soft sell, with a dab of crisp oversell thrown in here and there for effect.

1. The Hard Sell

Everyone's heard of the hard sell. It's for the chauvinist in all of us. The hard sell is the most attacking style of all. It's the one that, adopted early in an interview, will enable you to establish your independent professional authority. Its effectiveness lies in the relentless piling up of relevant technical detail about your past accomplishments: what you did, when you did it, what the consequences of your actions were, whom you worked for, what they thought of you.

The hard sell is no-nonsense selling. It's a style that conveys commitment and energy. With it, you are telling your prospect that he has something you want and you mean to get it. The hard sell never lets up. It's Joe Frazier in drag: center of the ring, crouching, left and right to the body, left and right to the head. The hard sell says: "I'm what you're looking for. This is where the search ends."

Case Study: Gerri Rosenthal, Graphic Design*

Gerri Rosenthal, born and raised on New York's Upper West Side, was perhaps the most audacious woman we interviewed. Twenty-nine, single, and the General Manager of a large graphic design studio, Gerri had pursued

---

*We have used this example of an internal promotion because the straight hard sell can be risky unless your prospect is either particularly tough or sufficiently well known to you that he will not be alienated by what might be interpreted as rudeness.

her goals with the single-minded drive of a fanatic. Her brief but, by most women's standards, dazzling career had led her through a miscellany of jobs: free-lance photography, print sales—she had even spent a few months selling used cars in the Bronx.

"I got this job," she said defiantly, "because I deserved it. And because I deserved it, I demanded it. And because I demanded it, I got it."

Gerri had joined the studio about three years earlier as a sales representative, merchandising the studio's facilities both to advertising agencies and to a variety of client companies needing such things as catalogues, brochures, in-house newsletters, and so forth.

"After about fifteen months of this," Gerri went on, "I'd pulled in over $1.5 million in billings for this operation. I was easily their best salesperson. I'd got to know the business inside out, so I asked the president of the company for a meeting to discuss my future here."

Prior to the discussion, Gerri prepared a complete analysis (on paper) of her achievements in the organization to date, plus a brief summary of her accomplishments before joining. In addition, she included an appendix to her written statement, outlining half a dozen strategies she believed the studio should adopt in order to achieve certain internal economies and to increase its rate of growth. As the coup de grâce, she had also written a letter of resignation that she was prepared to submit, on the spot, if her requirements were not met.

"In I went," she said, "one week after my twenty-seventh birthday, to tell my boss that the buck stopped here."

The negotiating session lasted two and three-quarter hours, during the course of which Gerri took the fight to her boss at all times. She pushed and probed and pressed.

"He told me I was too young. I said that I wasn't too young to secure $1.5 million of new business. Then he said

I hadn't been here long enough. I said I'd been here long enough to secure $1.5 million of new business. Then he said that the other employees would resent so rapid a promotion. 'Just like they resented the way the art department was refurbished six months ago as a result of the fact that, due to my efforts, this studio's billings were 35 percent higher than anticipated last fiscal year,' I replied."

Gerri's boss asked to be allowed to think about it. Gerri said that in her opinion the situation was cut and dried. Her boss said that she was a merciless Upper West Side hustler. She replied that, as far as she was concerned, he'd just furnished a further reason why she should be given what she wanted.

"Jesus Christ," said her boss, wildly.

"He can't help you," Gerri claims to have said. "He was into carpentry. We're into graphic design."

And that is an example of the hard sell: hard-hitting, inexorable. Like Gerri Rosenthal, you have to take control in the hard sell, never allowing the conversation to drift.

But be careful. Many men resent being subjected to the *female* hard sell. They feel hemmed in, patronized. Never lose sight of the fact that there are tens of thousands of apparently powerful men in business for whom the confident, aggressive, talented woman represents the ultimate threat. If at any time during your spiel you feel that you are turning your prospect off, switch styles. Backtrack from ring center, do an Ali shuffle, and slide into soft sell. Dance and weave until your prospect has regained his composure. Then start jabbing again, but with restraint. Try to build up a cautious round-by-round points lead.

Remember who's boss.

2. The Soft Sell

Cunning, defensive, mildly insidious, the soft sell is a ride-with-the-tide, go-with-the-flow approach. Somewhat cerebral and very civilized, the soft sell requires that instead of dominating you are (apparently) dominated. Your prospect does the talking and takes the initiative.

As in the hard sell, you are perfectly capable of piling up relevant technical details about your past accomplishments, but you do so only if the circumstances require. In the soft sell, your ability is somewhat taken for granted. The soft-sell interview is, more often than not, a kind of personality test.

Case Study: Alex Merrill, Sales Management

The contrast between Alex Merrill and Gerri Rosenthal could scarcely be more acute. It's restraint versus aggression, cool versus hot, Manhattan east versus Manhattan west. Yet, in its own way, each woman's approach is as successful as the other. Alex works for a multinational corporation, which manufactures and sells a wide variety of industrial and consumer goods: from carbon products and batteries to plastic ashtrays and garbage bags. Her background is academic rather than commercial, and her career lacks the sense of compelling urgency that characterizes Gerri Rosenthal's.

Alex was recruited to the company after a two-year period as a management trainee with one of that company's competitors. She applied for a position advertised in the *New York Times* and, in doing so, was subjected to what she privately conceded was "an annoying rigmarole" of meetings, discussions, lunches, and tests designed to determine her suitability.

"Once my basic credentials were confirmed and checked out," Alex explained, "and my serious interest in the job was established, I was asked to meet no fewer than six different people, only two of whom were directly involved in the job I was going to do. It was as if the company had a policy of vetting potential managers by using the managers of other divisions as human qualifying systems."

At one stage, Alex received a telephone call at home from one of the people who had interviewed her a week earlier, inviting her to "have a chat" with the woman who ran a part of the company in which she had not the slightest interest. Bemused, she met with her a couple of days later. Everything was very casual, very informal. "I was so fed up with the whole business that, early on in this discussion, I made the mistake of indulging in a scarcely camouflaged yawn."

But, as Alex observed, "these lateral meetings have a vital role to play in final hiring decisions. They're cumbersome, but crucial. What you have to do is recognize them for what they are: tests of character."

So Alex played the game.

Since there was no point in talking about her prospective job, she spent her time chatting about the corporation through which that job was being made available. She said how much she liked the atmosphere, the people, the sense of "controlled freedom" that the company appeared to offer (a brilliantly conceived self-contradiction that anyone applying for a corporate position would do well to remember: it addresses, simultaneously, the perceived virtues and vices of corporate life without suggesting any kind of damaging preference).

"This," Alex said, "was pure soft sell. No feminist stance-taking, no pushy rhetoric about the bottom line, no jarring references to the slowness of the corporate hiring process. Stay alert and be political. That's the way."

And the key word is *alert*. The soft sell never degenerates into mush. Remember, you are being observed. Your prospect may be trying to see just how malleable you are. Never let him feel entitled to conclude, after you've gone: "Too nice, that one. Bright. But too damn nice."

"The soft sell," Alex Merrill told us, "is like Bermuda. Unspoiled. Unhurried. Uncommon."

3. The Oversell

This is for gamblers. The oversell implies deliberate deception through the systematic inflation of your competence and experience. It promises what it rarely delivers. All surface rhetoric and little substance, the oversell is for the superambitious woman with intelligence and chutzpah. It's for the person who believes that a quick mind, adaptability, and a knack for talking herself out of the tightest of corners are the three necessary and sufficient conditions for any employment position. Experience, so the oversell argument goes, is an illusion. Bullshit can always be counted on to baffle brains.

The oversell should be adopted only as a last resort. Perhaps you are a secretary, trapped in the mind-numbing maw of an IBM Selectric, who would do almost anything to escape. Your business experience is limited but yourself are bright. Your present employer is resistant to the idea of promoting you. Something's got to give. A cleverly composed but evasive résumé has opened up a number of interesting doors, and so you decide to go for broke.

Preparation and verbal improvisation are the keys to the oversell. Anticipate being questioned on the principles and practices of whatever it is you are being interviewed to do, memorize the appropriate buzzwords of the business, and *come on strong*. Make abundant use of expressions like "involved with," "associated with," and "that was a project I worked on at the planning stage" (i.e., you typed the original proposal). Everything you say has to be delivered with complete authority and conviction.

If at any stage in your oversell your prospect discovers himself to be a victim of your deception, admit everything and then try to show that it is a testament to your enterprise, imagination, and nerve that you have managed to get so far without being found out.

4. Hard Selling with a Soft-Sell Style

Finally, the jugular squeezed by a calfskin glove: hard selling with a soft-sell style. Beautiful to observe, this selling
strategy is reserved for selling's superstars. It's the toughest to perfect, the toughest to resist. The most flexible of
selling approaches, the smoothest, and the one most appropriate (we think) to the female job hunter, hard selling
with a soft-sell style combines the best features of hard
and soft selling: it's direct and relentless yet self-effacing
and apparently casual.

Case Study: Judith Belgrave, Magazine Marketing

Judith Belgrave had been in the magazine business for
about eight years. Having begun at the bottom rung (selling magazine subscriptions by telephone), she had gradu-
ally developed her experience and skills in several different directions: advertising sales, media research, circulation promotion. She was, in short, a top-notch magazine
generalist; someone who could be counted on to deliver
high-class commercial work with little or no supervision.
Her ambition was to work for a major national magazine,
preferably in New York—which is where, as anyone in
magazines knows, the action is.

So Judith, who had spent most of her time in Chicago,
started investigating opportunities in Manhattan. She
tried them all, from *The New Yorker* through *Rolling Stone*
to the newsweeklies. Her résumé contained the right combination of accomplishment-oriented buzzwords, her
track record was memorable, and her presence in interviews was, as she herself said, "pleasantly precocious and
very much to the point."

As is so often the case in the job hunt, pure persistence
paid off in the end, and she aroused active interest at one
of the big publishing corporations whose most prominent
magazine property was an internationally respected business weekly. During the course of a "single punishing day

in June" Judith had discussions with a personnel executive, the magazine's advertising director, its publisher, its
research manager, and, finally, an inscrutable recruitment
consultant whom the corporation appeared to use as a
kind of fail-safe psychological checking mechanism and
who subjected her to what she denounced to us as "various simplistic tests."

"I've never in my life had so many classy conversations
in one day," Judith said. "At the end of it all I met with the
divisional vice-president who said that I seemed to have
impressed a lot of people in the organization—to which I
replied that a lot of people in the organization had impressed me, a remark which I felt combined tact with aggression in just about acceptable proportions."

As Judith pointed out, the higher up the corporate lad-
der you go, the less acceptable it is to be overtly opportunistic. The emphasis is on easy, patrician elegance supported by a quiet but unmistakable sense of purpose.

"If I do say so myself, I put on a magnificently controlled display for this guy. I went over the projects I'd
worked on, the sales I'd made, the decisions I felt I'd influenced. I made my remarks relevant, bottom-line oriented,
but essentially throwaway. If a decision I'd made contributed $80,000 to the profit of a magazine I worked on, I said
so—but in a manner that suggested the achievement was
essentially routine, everyday. And when he asked if I had
any questions, I said that yes, I did have one or two. Then,
as if making them up as I went along, I put five carefully
prepared, very specific ones to him: the first about the
corporation's recent acquisition of a group of radio sta-
tions in Illinois; the second about the circulation growth
of a particular magazine I knew he was responsible for;
the third about where I could expect to be in three years'
time if I joined the company; the fourth about the personalities of a few of the people I would be working with in
the event that I was hired; the fifth about his perception of

the role the flagship publication of the company played in the international business community."

The point about Judith Belgrave's performance (and it *was* a performance) is that beneath the surface poise she tried to exhibit a business mentality that was well prepared, acute, and effortlessly knowledgeable. Hard selling with a soft-sell style is for use with your most important prospects. Adopt it as you canter effortlessly down the backstretch during the last lap of your job hunt. But be careful. Practice.

There is a book to be written about the schizophrenia of selling. The book would show how and why it is that much of the most brilliant selling is done by people who are accessible and frank on the one hand, and opportunistic and evasive on the other. Yet that's what you, the top-job hunter, have to be at this, the most difficult, delicate, and dangerous stage of your campaign: a study in controlled schizophrenia, making shrewd, imperceptible adjustments between rectitude and self-consideration.

10

THE INTERVIEW

TOP-JOB INTERVIEWS are not often friendly. Neither are top-job interviewers, though they may appear to be on the surface. In fact, the higher up the business hierarchy you climb, the less likely you are to be interviewed (in the traditional sense of that word) at all. You will engage in apparently genial and composed discussions whose outer informality disguises a scrupulous exercise in personal assessment. Strip away the social proprieties and you are left with a primitive, ritualized tribal confrontation, one which involves the mutual manipulation of firmly held self-interests. Be coldly realistic about this. Most men are.

Keep in mind that the kind of person you are likely to have to persuade to hire you is a wily corporate pro. Competence will impress him, but not that much more than worldliness, self-assurance, and realism.

Here is where the percentage play pays off. Candidate tension and self-doubt rise in direct proportion to the *lack* of employment opportunities. But not in your case. Moving coolly against concurrent fronts, your confidence is sustained by several fall-back positions. Prepared and packaged, promoted and pretested (that's what all those early nonessential meetings are about), you *know* you are one of the hottest properties to hit the employment market in five years. Hang loose, glide.

Think tough. At least during the last day or two before you start attending serious meetings. Have someone whose cynicism and business acumen you trust (you might even decide to use your genial neighborhood headhunter) go over your résumé and fire some hard questions at you. Get that person to play fast and loose with your accomplishments: attacking, probing, putting down. Keep in mind that somewhere out there, lying in wait for you, is a grizzled old pro who will rip your claims about yourself to shreds. Defend yourself, ahead of time, against that possibility with a few dry runs. Be prepared to:

1. Identify and discuss in detail the kinds of projects you worked on and what the precise consequences of your involvement were.
2. justify your employment history, especially in terms of moving from one job to another, with carefully propounded (even if you have to invent a few of them) reasons.
3. Express your career goals convincingly, preferably on the basis of a three-to-five year timetable.
4. Rebut impertinent (and illegal) questions about marriage plans, age, intention to procreate, and domestic arrangements while you work. Title VII of the American Civil

Rights Act of 1964, as amended by the Equal Opportunity
Act of 1972, prohibits interviewers from asking you:
• about your marital status
• how many children you have
• whether you are pregnant
• how you feel about pregnancy and children

The same questions are prohibited by Canadian
Human Rights Commission guidelines for organizations
under federal jurisdiction. For regulations governing private employers, consult the Human Rights Commission of
the province involved.

Questions along these lines represent an unnecessary
intrusion into your private life and are irrelevant to your
professional preoccupations.

Say so.

Keep your eyes peeled, your ears pricked up before key
interviews. Look for clues, even as you wait in the lobby
for your meetings. Get a feel for the atmosphere of the
company you are visiting, the people, the receptionist and
the manner in which she addresses you. Eavesdrop dis-
creetly on snatches of conversation. Assess the level of
formality with which employees address one another.
Note how secretaries are treated—with brusque indiffer-
ence, paternalistic concern, or proper respect.

Try to develop early insights about the person
scheduled to interview you. Does your prospect receive
you promptly? Lack of punctuality suggests one of four
things: exceptional busyness (a good sign); a power-play
mentality (a bad sign—power plays are for corporate in-
fighting, not interviewing newcomers); disorganization or
carelessness; or, finally, downright insecurity (disastrous).
Observe the manner in which you are received: in person,
or through a secretary. It's a surefire sign of a loser if an

interviewer with an unprepossessing office feels the need to send a secretary out to fetch in callers.

Bear in mind that an interview starts the moment your arrival is announced, not later when you cross the threshold of your prospect's office. It's astonishing (and more than a little frightening) to consider what some high-ranking people perceive as being significant personality indicators. One headhunter we interviewed talked at length about the preinterview ploys he used to make early candidate assessment: the magazines people picked up (as an indication of their intellectual proclivities), and the chairs they chose. "Valerie, our receptionist," this particular headhunter went on gleefully, "plays an important role in our candidate assessment program. Ever watchful, Valerie. Don't know what we'd do without her."

But Valerie, and all the other Valeries like her, can be fooled. How? Easy. Having taken your seat in the reception area—or even in your prospect's office if, once he's invited you to enter, he steps out and keeps you waiting—remove your own magazine from your briefcase and read it. Carry something flashy and unusual (*Women's Wear Daily* is a chic insider's choice, far subtler than *Vogue*). For a big business meeting, flaunt a recent issue of *The Economist*—a much less proletarian periodical than *Business Week* or, heaven forbid, *Time*. Don't make the corny mistake of taking reading matter appropriate to the nature of the job under discussion, e.g., the *New York Times Book Review* for an interview at a publisher's. Something idiosyncratic is better; perhaps a special-interest magazine reflecting one of your private enthusiasms. Beware of being thought of as ingratiating.

Once inside your prospect's office, choose your seat carefully. Look for the second most powerful place to settle in (unless, of course, your choice is made for you), and slip into it gracefully. Faced with the choice between a single chair and a sofa, choose the latter. Don't appropriate a high, stiff-backed wing chair. It's there for a purpose. And that purpose is fulfilled only when your prospect is sitting in it gazing laconically down at you.

Let your prospect lead, especially during those vital early intuitive seconds of the meeting. Imagine that your prospect is a rather successful, professionally accomplished maiden aunt who, out of a distant interest in your personal development, has invited you for tea at her apartment. Behave towards your prospect as your aunt would almost certainly expect you to behave towards her: with a discreet mixture of controlled warmth and unassuming respect.

Engage a mental version of "cruise control" while those early commonplace exchanges are being covered. Direct at least 20 percent of your intellectual attention towards physical fact-finding: office decor, your prospect's clothes, arrangement of furniture. Make a fast, common-sense interpretation of the miscellany of external symbols that help define the business personality of the person you are meeting. Deep leather chairs, reproduction walnut desks and oriental carpets, for example, speak of a preoccupation with grandeur, traditional values, and largesse. Glass, chrome, and modern graphics suggest fastidiousness, clarity of mind, and parsimony.

Pleasantries dealt with, go, urbanely, with the flow. That first transition, from the conversational to the professional, tells all. The range and variation of interview procedures women encounter are more complex and demanding than those met by men. Beyond having to deal with routine questions about background and technical ability, female candidates for particular job opportunities are frequently subjected to mild forms of harassment. Our research (and considerable personal experience) suggests that, broadly speaking, there are seven different kinds of interview, ranging from the routine fact-finding exercise right along to the business lunch. At least two of the interview formats we have isolated (Big Daddy and Just a Gigolo) are, in our view, unique to women; the remainder are common to both sexes:

1. Down the Line
2. Trick or Treat
3. Big Daddy
4. Just a Gigolo
5. Ménage à Trois
6. Out to Lunch
7. Only Cartesians Need Apply

1. Down the Line

The straightforward informational kind of interview, one that seemingly amounts to little more than a routine checking of your personal and professional background, is frequently misunderstood by women. Naïvely, they tend to believe that apparently honest, dispassionate-sounding questions deserve equally honest, dispassionate-sounding responses. But the politics of the recruitment process suggest that this kind of interview has to be treated not as an exercise in epistemology, but rather as an opportunity for some subtle showing-off.

There is, by way of illustration, an illuminating and useful anecdote surrounding the first read-through (when the cast sits in a rehearsal room and "reads through" the text of the play going into production) of John Dexter's sensational production of *Othello* in 1964. Laurence Olivier, who was playing the title role, decided to introduce a surprising and wholly effective new element into the proceedings. As Kenneth Tynan put it: "Normally on these occasions the actors do not exert themselves. They sit in a circle and mumble, more concerned with getting to know one another than with giving a performance. Into this polite gathering Olivier tossed a hand-grenade. He delivered the works—a fantastic, full-volume display."* The consequence of this highly unexpected initiative was to establish the credentials (as if they needed to be established) of the central personality in the play right at the outset. And it also indicated that Olivier's prerehearsal preparation was exhaustive.

Our suggestion is that you consider a diluted form of the interviewing equivalent of Olivier's ploy in those ostensibly procedural Down the Line discussions that frequently precede more serious employment talks. Try, right at the beginning, to put some distance between yourself and other candidates.

Be different. Shine.

"The secret with these routine interviews is to regard them as personality tests. Don't get bogged down with too much detail. Tell the interviewer accurately and snappily what he wants to hear—about yourself, your background, why you're interested in the job. Keep the delivery upbeat and fresh. The fact is that summarizing personal and career details in an interview is the easiest thing in the world to do. Okay. So recognize that. And put everything you've got into verbal presentation. But don't be cute."

Nancy Mayer knows what she's talking about. She works in the personnel department of a major Fifth Avenue retailer, interviewing hundreds of people a year in her job. She talks to women applying not only for secretarial and sales jobs but also for more senior positions in sales and general management. Many of her interviews are of the routine, fact-finding kind—exploring the when, what, and where of an employment history, prior to a can-

---

*From Tynan's book *The Sound of Two Hands Clapping*.

didate's going forward to more detailed discussions with line managers.

"Very occasionally," Nancy told us, "I get to meet a young woman who turns me on during one of these exercises. Those that do turn me on—and remember I can do these interviews in my sleep—tend to have three characteristics in common. First, they're not afraid to be direct and warm. They look me in the eye and, believe it or not, they smile.[*] Second, they're prepared to be humorous in the right places. I ask a routine question, they recognize it for what it is and respond with a sense of irony and fun about the thing. That's fine. It means they're alive, thinking. We don't hire people who appear to have just been lobotomized. Third, and this is very important, they take the trouble to give the impression that their job moves follow some kind of logic, that there's some kind of rhyme and reason to what they want to do. I can't stand it when women come to me and say, 'Gee. I just think it'll be a blast working here.' And some do say that, you know."

Think of the Down the Line interview as an opportunity to define and determine, quite apart from your basic occupational resources, a group of selling propositions about your character and personality that make you different from the competition. Since in the basic recruitment scheme of things women are still very much regarded as number twos, they have but one alternative: to try harder.

2. Trick or Treat

The principal difference between the Down the Line and the "Trick or Treat" interview is one of psychological and

---

*More than one personnel executive we spoke to said that the problem with many women is that they take interviews too *seriously*. It's a serious business, to be sure, but that doesn't mean it's grim!

intellectual intensity. The former is, in principle anyway, "coastable." The latter is all sudden inclines, blind curves, and unexpected changes of pace. You are, at Trick or Treat time, on trial. The interviewer, though pleasant on the surface, will probe your background and experience with great resolution and incisiveness. If there is a chink in your armor he will pierce it and, unless you maintain an impeccable facade, coolly watch you bleed.

During the Trick or Treat interview, your interviewer is quite likely to pick up on what you consider to be your finest and most clear-cut achievement, and belittle it. You may have been responsible for a $150,000 export deal or involved with a pivotal company economy or acquisition. No matter. Trick or Treat interviewers are more interested in personal or professional analysis than in any particular sense of self-worth their prey might have. Look at the Trick or Treat interview as a kind of *viva voce* examination. Your résumé is a thesis whose contents you are under an obligation to defend. The quality of your defense will determine, in the eyes of your questioner, the value of your professional achievements. So when the observation is made "It seems to me that even though you claim to have done such and such, it is rather less significant than you would want people to believe"—be prepared to fiercely argue the point, stressing, in particular, the value of your accomplishment *within the context in which it was made.* In other words, claim that under the circumstances your achievement was, without question, important and original.

One woman we spoke to told us how the size of the budgets she was responsible for managing while working for a Canadian company operating out of Vancouver was ridiculed by a man interviewing her for a job in Los Angeles. Her response was cut and dried. She said, rightfully, that since markets in Canada were ten times smaller than those in the United States, an intellectually honest appraisal of her performance by him would mean that every financial statement made in her résumé ought to be multiplied tenfold. "As a matter of fact," she told us, "it was pure chance that I was able to hit him with such a solid rejoinder. It so happened that my boyfriend drove me to the interview and, en route, fired a succession of tough questions at me. One was a version of the question I was actually asked. Homework helps."

Case Study: Patricia Hadley, Advertising

This was not so much an interview as an exercise in arrogant self-aggrandizement on the part of the interviewer. A meeting with the "Electric Eel" (the nickname of a particularly fierce research director at a prominent advertising agency in New York) was the last in a long line of interviews that Patricia Hadley endured during the culmination of a major job-hunting effort in 1977. The department of the agency she hoped to join was, as it happened, dominated by women.

Her first meeting was with the Electric Eel's "number two," whom Patricia managed to satisfy on the elementary level of background, technical qualifications, and basic career ambitions. This particular woman also delivered what Patricia privately felt was a dissertation on the need for people joining the department to "fit in temperamentally" with the personalities of the people already there. On number two's recommendation, Patricia was invited to spend the following day at the agency in order to have the opportunity to meet the other senior members of the department. As Patricia said: "'Opportunities to meet' other members of a particular department you are hoping to join are, in effect, an additional series of interviews. Though they may appear to be semi-social occasions, it's a serious mistake to treat them as such. A false move in one of these little get-togethers can damage your chances irreparably."

The trick is to appear to take these "interviewettes" at their face value, while simultaneously restraining the entirely natural tendency to "open up" when in the presence of a potential colleague who (apparently) wants nothing more out of life at that moment than to get to know you better. Be careful: your worst enemy in situations like these is unbridled loquacity.

Next on the list was the Electric Eel herself. And it was here that Patricia made a mistake.

Interviews require two kinds of preparation: intellectual and psychological. The first has to do with the act of pulling together and reviewing, prior to a particular meeting, the facts about your employment history and the manner in which you have assembled and presented them in what is often (as in this case) a succession of prior interviews. The second has to do with the establishment of a mental defense against unanticipated pressure in what may (as in this case) appear at first to be a formality'.

"Right up to minutes before I was due to see her, final meeting was promoted by everyone, including the departmental receptionist whom I'd inevitably got to know quite well by then, as entirely routine. I was in. The Electric Eel was going to give me a friendly once-over. Well, that's not what happened. I sat down in front of her and, without any kind of introduction, I was subjected to a long and demanding interrogation. I was picked up like a piece of cold beef and put through the meat grinder. As it happened, she'd called my former boss and found out exactly what he thought of me, particularly of my weaknesses. And those were what she went after."

Patricia came through. But only just. And not before it had been amply demonstrated to her that she had technical deficiencies in her background that were understood by the most powerful person in the department she hoped to join, an operational reality with which she would have to deal every day of her future working life there.

Her postmortem on the meeting was this: "While there wasn't a damn thing I could have done about the criticisms of my lack of competence in certain areas, I should have been able to defend myself more thoroughly against the unintentional impression I gave that I was largely unaware of it. I didn't think. I didn't prepare. I wasn't self-critical enough all the way through to the end. I went into the meeting with my guard down, and nearly blew it. At the very least, I was presented with the chance to claim that I wanted the job so much precisely because it gave me a way of strengthening a part of my background that was admittedly weak"—a conclusion that Patricia would have been better advised to reach before crossing the Electric Eel's threshold.

3. Big Daddy

Big Daddy comes in two varieties: the paternalist and the soothsayer. In an interview encounter the latter is likely to be the more helpful of the two, for the soothsayer at least is capable of understanding you and your ambition on the only terms that count, those you have set for yourself. The paternalist sees you as an attractive stereotype, a fascinating version of the daughter he either has or has always wanted.

Much has been made of the role that certain kinds of sympathetic older men can play in the careers of young, ambitious women. The soothsayer (or rabbi, as he is sometimes called), identifiable by his honest enthusiasm for the energetic and intelligent efforts that you are evidently making to find yourself a job, is an interviewer whom it is least necessary for you to make a contrived effort to impress.

One woman we spoke to, working for a federal agency in Washington involved with developing financial aid programs for the Third World, observed that the secret with the soothsayer interview is that there is no secret. "Frankness and clarity of career intentions are what work in this kind of interview," she said. "Games, ploys, and stratagems are inappropriate. Just tell him what you've done and what you'd like to do. True to his nickname, he'll tell you whether your ambitions are realistic, and, if he takes to you, he'll also help you achieve them."

No such luck with the paternalist. In fact, of all the interview situations you encounter, the one involving him is least likely to bear fruit. It would be wonderful if we were able to recommend a list of stratagems that would enable a female interviewee to turn the tables on a dyed-in-the-wool paternalist. But we can't—not quite. Paternalism, particularly towards women, is one of the most profoundly entrenched attitudes in corporate life. Like a debilitating disease, paternalism can only be treated by the sustained use of appropriate medication: first-class work presented unambiguously as your own. However, while this approach makes sense once you have a job, it is clearly irrelevant in a situation where you are trying to secure one.

One woman we interviewed (Elayne Bernay, Research Director of *Ms.* magazine) was convinced that there is nothing you can do about overt paternalism in an interview situation. "We don't hire our children," she said bluntly. Another executive woman with whom we discussed the problem did have one recommendation. She referred to Disraeli's famous remark about the reason behind his successful political and personal relationship with Queen Victoria: "Everyone likes flattery; and when you come to royalty you should lay it on with a trowel," and observed that the word *paternalists* was a fitting replacement for the word *royalty*. In other words, she advised that you unabashedly flatter your prospect into submission. "Tell him that the central reason the job interests you is the opportunity to learn through the example and under the guidance of someone (namely him) whose reputation is of the highest order."

This statement puts your prospect in a double bind. He can only disagree with you at the risk of publicly diminishing his professional standing (and paternalists, like queens, rarely do that); or he can agree, in which case you have furnished him with a reason, over and above whatever hard qualifications support your candidacy, to take you more seriously than he did at the beginning of the meeting. Even if the paternalist sees through your soft soap, chances are that he will still be sufficiently impressed to offer you half a dozen referrals. If he doesn't, ask for them.

At this stage you have nothing to lose.

4. Just a Gigolo

The sexual harassment of women is extremely pervasive at all levels of working life. And there is no indication that it diminishes the higher up the socioeconomic scale one goes. It becomes subtler perhaps but, according to at least two contemporary treatments of the subject (*The Secret Oppression: Sexual Harassment of Working Women* by Constance Backhouse and Leah Cohen, and *Sexual Shakedown: The Sexual Harassment of Women on the Job* by Lin Farley), no less prevalent.

While the meretricious male chauvinist is more likely to badger you once you've been hired—and you therefore have more to lose—he's by no means averse to pick-up attempts during job interviews. Since sexual harassment will probably take place in the privacy of an office, you have very fragile empirical grounds on which to lodge a complaint to the interviewer's superior, if you decide to do so. No Civil Rights Act can protect you from sexual innuendo expressed behind closed doors.

Just a Gigolo comes in all shapes and sizes. But if he has a single, characteristic feature it is narcissism, a rabid self-love that, properly handled, can be turned very much to your advantage.

First, however, a warning. More than one headhunter we spoke to observed that occasionally a male interviewer, professionally concerned about how a female interviewee might react to possible sexual "come-ons" on the job (particularly if she were applying for a sensitive sales position, for example, involving frequent client meetings), might try to "test" his candidate in a manner that did not accurately reflect his own intentions. Our reaction to this (and, incidentally, the reaction of a number of women with whom we discussed the example) was that in most cases it represented a retrospective attempt at self-justification by an interviewer who got fresh and was rebuffed. Genuine or simulated, any attempt at sexual harassment has to be handled sternly. The response "My understanding is that this was intended to be a business meeting. I'm not prepared to respond to any questions or suggestions that bear on my personal life unless they are clearly relevant to the subject under discussion" is probably the most appropriate because:

- It serves notice that you take exception to his line of questioning.
- It is vague on the issue of whether or not the interviewer is deliberately testing you, therefore giving him an opportunity to backtrack.
- It gives the interviewer a chance to proceed on a civilized basis in a way that a straight "Listen, buster, this is a place of business not a singles' bar" does not.
- It works on men of all ages, from the pubescent stud to the middle-aged lecher.

A straightforward reprimand always beats moral indignation. It's more worldly, less ambiguous. Prissy people lack class. However, it's one thing to finesse a pass;

it's another to work for the man who made it. Remember, you'll be seeing a lot of this man if he hires you.

5. Ménage à Trois

It's two against one. Mr. X and Mr. Y. One asks the questions, the other sits there, watching, listening, and maybe taking notes. The atmosphere is formal, subdued, and almost alarmingly polite. It's like being back in the classroom.

The very artificiality of the situation is the reason that the Ménage à Trois interview is the trickiest for a candidate to come through unscathed. The political chemistry of the meeting can very easily get confused, particularly if the relative status of your two interrogators has not been made plain. For some women, used to full-scale sales presentations that oblige them to address several people simultaneously, the Ménage à Trois interview will present few problems. But for the rest, it can be downright terrifying.

And a terrified candidate, like a terrified actress, stands a better than average chance of flubbing her lines.

We spoke to one uncharacteristically helpful and conscientious headhunter who spent a great deal of her time and energy preparing her candidates for interviews. She offered advice, she told us, on résumé layout and design, copy writing, dress, and, most important, interview tactics. Over the years she had built up an extensive filing system about her various clients, a system based both on personal, first-hand judgments and also on reports from those of her candidates who had met with these clients. We raised the issue of the two-against-one interview and asked if she had any advice to offer candidates, particularly women, confronted with such a situation.

"Absolutely," she said. "The two-on-one interview, as you call it, can be very unnerving and counterproductive, in my view. I have a couple of clients, though, who feel it to be a proper part of the recruitment procedure, and they do it frequently. They either double up a line manager with someone from personnel, or, if they have more than one opportunity available in different divisions, they may set the thing up between the two appropriate managers and cut out personnel altogether. I tell my candidate to try to do three things in these cases: (a) establish the relative seniority of the people doing the interview so you can at least have a crack at impressing the more powerful; (b) address your answers to *both* parties, switching your attention from one to the other, so that neither feels left out; and (c) try to create a discussion-group atmosphere rather than that of a tribunal."

This particular headhunter suggested that the proportion of time spent addressing your answers to one or the other of your interviewers depends on who asks the question. If Mr. X asks the question, approximately two-thirds of your attention should be directed to him, the remaining one-third to Mr. Y. This tactic results in all three individuals, X, Y, and yourself, feeling fully involved in the discussion. If the interview shows signs of being dominated by one interviewer, it makes sense for you to fly a few interrogative trial balloons in the direction of the interviewer who says less. "If you've submitted a particularly detailed answer to one question," the headhunter said, "casually ask the second interviewer whether or not he agrees. Or suggest perhaps that you may have overlooked certain possible nuances, and invite him to fill them in."

The headhunter went on to say that if the quieter of the two interviewers remains unresponsive, you have no alternative but to return to a straight question-and-answer session with the more talkative of the two. "But at least you've tried to get outside the straitjacket. And that shows determination, originality, and strength of character, three very definite pluses."

6. Out to Lunch

There are three major tactical considerations for the job-related lunch: eat little, drink less, and stay alert to leading questions. An invitation to lunch is a further test, not a certificate of approval. While it suggests that your candidacy is being taken seriously (your prospects are prepared to invest some money in you), it certainly does not mean that you have been accepted and that further discussions are a formality.

In many ways the job-related lunch is the most demanding of all interview situations in which to perform well. Apart from being subjected to routine restaurant distractions (sudden outbursts of laughter, the clink of glasses), you are also obliged to juggle menus, cutlery, a napkin, the timing of your next mouthful.

The business lunch can be a trying affair, even for people who undertake it routinely. "Nevertheless," observed one former Hollywood agent we interviewed in Toronto, "there are rules. Believe me. I've breakfasted, brunched, and lunched my way into a zillion deals over the years and I know, I hope, *exactly* what they are."

While our contact was not specifically concerned about discussing the problems associated with the job-related lunch, the observations she made are entirely appropriate to it.

- Order something simple or something you know. Don't use the lunch as a culinary experiment. Choose forkable food. An attempt to negotiate a bowl of spaghetti, for example, could be disastrous.
- Have no more than one drink. Order a white wine spritzer, something light, anyway. Keep in mind, especially if you had no breakfast, that a drink unaccompanied by food will loosen your tongue faster than a drink consumed while eating.

- Check everything checkable. Distractions distract, so cut them out; let the coat-checker deal with them.
- Don't equivocate when the time comes to order. Execute the task swiftly and surely. Stay away from the "shall I have this or shall I have that" syndrome.
- Don't forget that you're at a meeting where, coincidentally, food is being consumed; your primary task is to concentrate on the conversation.
- Be as attentive to your smoking habits as you are to your drinking habits. Smoking is increasingly unfashionable these days, especially among *men*. If you *must* smoke, at least ask the people with whom you are lunching whether they mind.

Our former Hollywood agent friend said that the best piece of advice she could give a young woman invited to attend a job-related discussion in a restaurant was this: "Out to lunch has two meanings in America. And we all know what the second one is."

7. Only Cartesians Need Apply

We have all been subjected to the philosophical interview. Introduced towards the end of a series of preliminary discussions, or, perhaps, at the conclusion of a long, single conversation, the philosophical interview begins with the preamble: "Tell me. Now we've covered the basics about your job, let's talk about the future of [if it's your specialty] the synthetic rubber industry. Our problem is this. One of the major applications of our product is the prevention of soil erosion. But soil erosion is a topographical characteristic of Third World countries whose politics are, in general, erratic. What do you think our corporate policy should be?"

More than a few candidates have lost a job opportunity because they were unequal to the task of discussing the long-term implications of their work. The response "To be perfectly frank, I've never felt comfortable theorizing about the future of the synthetic rubber industry. Speculation is for academics or astrologers, not me" is rarely sufficient to turn the line of questioning away onto more empirical ground. On the contrary, a declared reluctance to stargaze is the sign of a closed mind, of a parochial intellect.

Theory is the final stroke of the duster that brings a high sheen to what you know about what you do. And the fact is that the more senior and powerful your interviewer, the more he will want you to display a comprehensive, thoughtful understanding of the business you are in.

Case Study: Michele Chalmers, Political Opinion Polling

Michele Chalmers works in Chicago for one of North America's most prominent political polling organizations, a company whose clients include not only government agencies but individual politicians who, among other things, use polling techniques to discover how well they and their policies are perceived and understood by the people they were elected to represent.

"There is," Michele told us, "something of a fine line to be drawn between at least two approaches to most kinds of political research. And when I was being interviewed for this job, I had to be careful not to go overboard for one at the expense of the other."

Michele was a statistician by training, a factor that tended to invest her approach to polling with a higher than average degree of pure number-crunching. "But that's insufficient in this organization," she told us. "The statistical analysis of voter perceptions and intentions is only part of the polling story. You also have to understand the political issues and how those issues operate in people's lives. Percentages alone can never help a politician shape policy."

Michele's central weakness as a potential employee was isolated during her very first interview. "The intellectual background of the woman I met originally was in anthropology, not statistics. We talked for an hour at cross-purposes. I wanted to discuss arithmetic; she wanted to talk about roles. So, inevitably, the issue came up: what *was* my approach to political research?"

The interview came to an end and Michele was given the opportunity to go away and consider her position. The polling organization wanted to maintain the dialogue because Michele had impressed them with her technical grasp of quantitative polling principles, and a few days later she was invited to return for a second meeting with the same woman. The discussion was short. At the end of it, the woman gave Michele a confidential political research report that she was asked to read and, two days later, comment on at a third meeting.

The research report, Michele told us, contained considerably less statistical material than she had expected. On the contrary, it consisted of (1) direct quotation: individual representative responses to questions about politician A's perceived honesty, for example; and comparisons of those responses to those expressed about politician B, with whom politician A competed for votes; (2) an attempt to identify precise nuances in voter attitudes by seeking answers to different linguistic formulations of the same question; and (3) straight political analysis.

"I went back for my third interview with a very different understanding of political research," Michele said. "Political research ultimately involves an examination of the psyche of the electorate: its values, its beliefs, its feelings. It's not enough to be able to say that politician A has a ten-point lead over politician B and that that lead, translated into party advantage terms, yields a thirty-seat margin in the state senate. That was how I used to think. And I thought that way because I had never before taken the trouble to think deeply enough about what I was actually doing."

The lesson here is obvious. Never go into a major job interview without being prepared for some tough exchanges about basic approaches, basic philosophies. And if you feel uncertain about your strengths in this area, bone up fast. Talk to colleagues, go to the library. Top-job interviews rarely stop at technical qualifications. Being able to express a reasonably coherent overview of your subject can represent the difference between being passed over and being hired.

Concepts count.

In the Cartesian spirit of healthy skepticism and clarity of mind, we offer you a concluding checklist of the five general questions you are most likely to be asked during your interviews. Since very few questions asked in interviews are entirely unambiguous, we have provided each one with a parenthetical translation.

- Tell me a little bit about yourself.
  Translates to: How much trouble have you taken over your career? How well are you able to track your professional life?
- Why do you want to leave your current employer?
  Translates to: What is the nature of your dissatisfactions and how rationally and coherently are you able to express them?
- What do you know about us?
  Translates to: Have you done your homework?
- Tell me about your current job.
  Translates to: Give me a concisely expressed summary of your present responsibilities in a way that enables me to see how your current work will have applications here.
- What do you think of your current management?

Translates to: To what extent are your present dissatisfactions likely to be duplicated here?

And, finally, we list below five working precepts to take with you into *all* your interviews.

1. If there's a silence, don't fill it. Let the interviewer fill it with a further question to which you can deliver a crisp, relevant answer.
2. Never leave a weakness unqualified.
3. Never leave a strength unsold.
4. Don't pass up an opportunity to ask a question.
5. Avoid talking about the redeeming social value of your profession, even if it has one.

The trouble with so many individuals involved in the recruitment process is that they have a natural, human aversion to rejecting people. This means that, unless brought firmly up against the issue, they will prefer prevarication to frankness. It's hard to look someone in the eye and tell her she is not going to make it. Far harder than a regretful telephone chat or, less upsetting still, than sending a tactful note.

The point of an interview is to proceed further. Better to provoke a turndown in a sequence of interviews by asking outright about your chances of success than to risk wasting time and energy pursuing the unpursuable.

One of your most formidable foes, at least during the interview stage of your campaign, is false hope. Your conviction that you have been outstandingly impressive in an interview is worthless without the interviewer's corresponding conviction that he wants to either continue the dialogue or make you an offer.

An offer closed is the job hunter's equivalent to a sale made. That comes next.

11

CLOSING TACTICS

CLOSE YOUR CAMPAIGN
as you opened it: alert to op-
portunities, attentive to detail. Be frank, be forthright, be
fair. Concentrate. Drawing that bottom line requires clarity of mind, clearness of eye, and firmness of hand. Pop the
cork when the ink is dry on an employment contract or a
letter of appointment, not before.

With some reason, employers have come to expect
women to be significantly less scrupulous and thorough
than men when it comes to negotiating the final details of
a job offer. Men have learned that the time to negotiate
their best deal is now, as they close, not later, after their

sale is made. Be ruthless with yourself on this issue. Take a deep breath, develop your position carefully, and be prepared to bargain.

"The art of negotiating," said a female vice-president we interviewed, "whether it's a TV-time buy or a salary for your next job, is to have the closest possible idea of what the best deal is you can make. Establish, in your mind, your minimum." You owe it to yourself, and to the sustained, imaginative effort you have made to get this far in your campaign, not to settle for a dime less either than you are worth or than a capable male would be offered.

A cleverly closed negotiation is a statement about your flexibility and, more important, your fiscal acumen. The extent to which you can demonstrate a directness of purpose about your own financial affairs is an employer's best guarantee that you will apply those same scrupulous standards to his.

And if he bitches about what a tough, demanding negotiator you are, tell him just that.

Closing begins when the routine questions have been resolved, when a clear mutual interest in pursuing the position under discussion has been established. Start closing when you're sure your prospect's hooked. Reel in slowly and deliberately. The bigger, stronger, more wily your quarry, the more subtly you must execute the landing process. In the give-and-take of closing, learn to recognize the breaking point. Look out for it. Anticipate it.

Talk money *early*. So many women (and plenty of men) are too diffident to establish, at the outset, what the salary range of the job under discussion is. Don't make that mistake. If the dollars aren't there, you are wasting time and energy chasing a dream. It's not necessary (in fact, it's tactically irresponsible) for you to establish precisely what you will be paid for a particular job, but you should at least discover the range.

If your prospect says he's paying between $20,000 and $23,000, and that sounds acceptable to you, smile, look earnest, and say, "Good. Because I had in mind between $22,000 and $25,000." It's a cute play because:

1. You go on record as being *inside* the salary ballpark.
2. You open up the possibility (unless your prospect is flatly resistant) of *upping* the salary ante.
3. Both parties can proceed confident that there ought not, at least *in the limited area of total compensation covered by a salary*, be major friction.

Negotiate salary in eighteen-month segments, at least. Don't allow your prospect to hide behind a flimsy smokescreen of undefined future raises. The remark "We'll take a look at what you're making six months down the road" should be balanced, flatly, by the suggestion that you prefer to talk about salary on a medium- to long-term basis. If your potential employer plays dumb, explain that a high-performance individual like yourself has discovered that one of the best ways to judge how well (or how badly) you are doing is by both the size and frequency of the increments you are offered. Suggest, for example, that if your starting salary is $20,000, it would not be unreasonable to expect that, provided you work very hard and perform exceptionally well, your salary might rise to *at least* $24,000 within two years (that's only 10 percent a year).

Induce your prospective employer to either:

1. endorse or (possibly) extend your prediction about likely raises, or
2. suggest alternatives

Once you have established a future twenty-four- or

eighteen-month salary goal, recommend a breakdown of the entire salary period into six-month intervals. On the basis of this example, you could then expect to receive raises of $1000 every six months. Failure to secure these raises, you might point out, would represent the clearest possible indication that you were not managing to perform at the mutually expected level. Under those circumstances, both parties could reexamine, and possibly terminate, the relationship.

The point is that prenegotiated raises offer both employer and employee a clear set of mutually understood public criteria for judging a successful employee performance. And, of course, a prenegotiated raise implies a high level of commitment to the company on your part. You're talking "futures" right at the beginning. That's a plus.

It may be that the principle of six-monthly increments conflicts with company salary policy—in which case you will have to prenegotiate on an annual basis. Or a potential employer may be doggedly resistant to the principle of prenegotiation at all. You will then have to make an independent decision about whether to proceed with that company at all. At the very least, try to negotiate your raises at a *minimum*, so that if the company you join does particularly well, you get more. Don't end up with a 6 percent raise if things go badly.

Get your numbers down on paper. Ahead of time. And negotiate with them in front of you. Take a calculator. Another woman we interviewed described a very tough closing negotiation she engaged in recently during which both parties had carefully assembled the details of their respective financial positions and bargained over them. "That's healthy," the woman said, "it's open, honest, and fun. It gave me enormous confidence in the guy who was hiring me. And my approach had the same effect on him."

And when a particular opportunity gets into the area of

what the cognoscenti might call "heavy bread," you would be wise to reach for the phone and dial your accountant. It's always worthwhile having an experienced money man around if and when you're lucky enough in the culmination of your job hunt to be talking top dollar.

But what do you do if you're uncertain about the salary you should demand, and your prospective employer is unforthcoming about what he has in mind? We've all engaged in the "you tell me"/"no, you tell me" salary game at least once in our lives.

Believe it or not, our best recommendation is that you call a couple of headhunters. At the very least, they can give you a clear idea of what you're worth. You can then, during a salary discussion with a prospective employer who tries the "you tell me" gambit, calmly cite industry averages to support the figure he forces you to present. If he refuses to buy the industry average, you may decide to allow a quizzical look to sweep across your face before declaring, "If you don't accept the industry average, you must have some prior notion of what the job under discussion is worth."

And there is really no answer to that. To the extent that continued evasion of the issue represents what you can expect from any and all future salary negotiations with this employer, you may decide to withdraw from the opportunity altogether. There is, in our experience, no better way to judge the sincerity, management style, and business competence of a prospective employer than by how a salary negotiation is handled. Bargaining is fine. There are two sides to every deal. But financial chicanery is unnecessary, unpleasant, and intellectually dishonest.

Case Study: Marie-Hélène Dupont, Export Finance

One of the smartest salary maneuvers to make in a closing situation was suggested to us by a woman we interviewed in Paris. Marie-Hélène Dupont works in export finance as the assistant to the chief accountant of a smallish trading company. We'd heard from mutual friends that Marie-Hélène had composed a brilliantly original résumé to win her current job. But our interest in her was heightened when she told us how she managed to beat out or, as she put it (rather more gracefully), *surclasser* the two men with whom she was competing for her present position.

"Employers," Marie-Hélène said, "love candidates with the courage of their convictions, particularly in sales. And, especially in France, so few women recognize the two-way nature of an opportunity."

As Marie-Hélène was anxious to stress, if an employer is prepared to gamble on you, why shouldn't you be prepared to gamble on an employer? So Marie-Hélène deliberately negotiated a *low* starting salary in order to receive a bigger six-months' raise. Coming in low on an initial salary request, provided it is clearly tied to reasonable future raises, can do wonders for how your prospective boss perceives you. But do get it down on paper. Such a stance tells that boss that you're tough, determined, unafraid to compete.

"In effect," said Marie-Hélène, 'I told my prospect that I was interested enough in the job itself to offset present against future gains." In a closing negotiation, there is no more convincing position to take.

Another situation in which a salary maneuver of this kind can pay off is when your candidacy is supported by a headhunter. Headhunters, as we have already explained, are compensated by the hirer, not you, the hiree. Often their fee can amount to *one-third* of your starting salary. As a general rule, that fee will be paid in installments, the last of which will not fall due until you have been at the job for six months. A low starting-salary request from you translates into a lower placement payment to the headhunter—an opportunity most employers find difficult to resist. Be candid. Point out this possibility to your prospective employer. Use it as an incentive to make him hire you. Not only can you use the lower fee to the headhunter as a closing leverage mechanism, you can also enjoy the quiet satisfaction of having hustled job-hunting's supreme hustlers.

There is more to a top job than straight salary. You must keep this crucial consideration in mind throughout your negotiations because, in the final analysis, money is just one part of *total compensation*. Depending on the seniority of the position under discussion, there are significant and often substantial individual elements to consider in a total compensation package. The ancillary benefits and perquisites available with respect to one job may outweigh the cash advantage with respect to another. Only you can decide which elements are most important to you. The mere act of *mentioning* the availability of company compensations can provoke an employer into offering them. Odds are that certain perquisites are routinely offered to male employees of similar rank to you. But, with almost frightening frequency, women are not told about them. Once you are offered (or are certain you're about to be offered) a job, ask for a complete description of the compensation package that goes along with that job. The more senior the position, the more complex the package is likely to be. So, to be safe, do what a man would do under comparable circumstances: take notes.

Don't forget that business is built on compromise, on the idea that to every offer there is a counteroffer; that for the giveable there is, potentially, the takeable too. People (employers especially) are prepared to go to enormous lengths to get something they want; the trick is to discover how far a job offerer will extend himself in order to secure your services, and then (within the constraints of tact and reason) to press him to the limit. Most women have *no idea* of the range of advantage that can be squeezed out of a properly prepared closing.

What follows is an attempt to isolate and summarize the components that constitute total compensation. Obviously, not every job offer will involve all twenty-one of the items mentioned here. Our purpose in listing and explaining them is to provide you with a framework around which to organize your closing negotiation.

MONEY

1. Salary
2. Bonus schemes
3. Commissions
4. Stock options: the right to buy common shares in a company, usually at a predetermined price and quantity
5. Profit sharing: a system whereby designated employees are entitled to a share of a company's profits
6. Deferred profit sharing: as above, except that monies due are held in trust and may only be withdrawn with the consent of both employer and employee (at which time they are taxable, not before)

BENEFITS

7. Health insurance
8. Pension plan
9. Dental plan
10. Vacations

PERQUISITES

11. Expense account
12. Credit cards
13. Club memberships

14. Company products, available free or at cost
15. Automobile: subject to wide variation and conditions, ranging from total availability, i.e., provision of vehicle, insurance, and contribution to running costs; to simply an allowance, i.e., an agreement to pay for gas and mileage on company-related business
16. Parking: free or subsidized space

STATUS

17. Size and location of office
18. Use of secretary (private or shared)
19. How the industry as a whole perceives the company*
20. How the industry as a whole will perceive your position (your title and functions) within the company*
21. How the company itself will perceive your position within its hierarchy

Essentially, most job offers involve a mixture of four separate but related ingredients: money, benefits, perquisites, and status.

The incredible fact is that, other than 7, 8, and 9, issues 1 through 18 are all *negotiable*. They represent thirteen separate bargaining chips that the canny female job hunter has at her disposal. Of the negotiable issues some are, needless to say, more negotiable than others. Leaving aside 1 as the most obviously negotiable of all, the remaining potent issues are (2) bonus schemes, (3) commissions, (10) vacations, (11) expense account, (15) automobile, (16) parking, (17) size and location of office, and (18) use of secretary.

For those of you unaccustomed to the (sometimes) theatrical quality of a tough bargaining session, we offer this advice: *don't take yourself too seriously*. Be good-

---

*Not to be discussed with your employer but to be part of your private deliberations.

humored, adaptable, and, above all, worldly. In our view, a woman confronted with a compensation package involving items 2, 3, 4, 5, 6, 11, and 15 ought to consult with an accountant prior to a closing discussion in order to accurately assess how they relate to (and modify, perhaps substantially) item 1. An accountant can provide a clear idea of the relative value of each issue and, almost certainly, which (if any) are least dispensable.

Then, in a thoroughly businesslike fashion, using the notes you have taken throughout your negotiations, type yourself a list of what you perceive to be the key elements of the company's final offer. Take care to relate them systematically to the *minimum* terms you would accept. During your final meetings, invite the person with whom you are closing the opportunity to review the list in order to ascertain that both of you have a clear understanding of the offer.

At this stage of closing, you will be either presented with a letter of appointment or asked to sign an employee contract (normally a detailed summary of standard corporate benefits and entitlements, together with additional clauses regarding severance arrangements, and a stipulation binding the employer to retain you for a given length of time). Make sure that the mutually agreed upon elements from the list you typed up are plainly itemized in the letter or contract. If they aren't, insist that they be included. Your rigorous attention to the details of a final offer will rarely be interpreted by an employer as defensiveness or a lack of confidence in his financial integrity.

Case Study: Lorraine Greif, Cosmetics Industry

A few years ago a woman executive at Revlon was approached by the Helena Rubinstein corporation about a major job opportunity. While very enthusiastic about the prospective position, the woman had problems perceiving how far the company would go to meet her compensation requirements. Her husband, with characteristic male ag-gressiveness, believed that she owed it to herself to bar-gain for a great, rather than simply a good, deal. In par-ticular, he urged her, since at that time Helena Rubinstein had offices on Long Island and they lived in Manhattan, to persuade the company to make a large contribution to the monthly cost of the automobile they were currently leas-ing and which she would have to use daily to get to her office. The woman told her husband flatly that Helena Rubinstein would never go for it. "If they seriously wish to hire you, they will," he replied. In support of his view, and to help her in her negotiations, he had her consult with his lawyer, his accountant, and even his actuary. Armed to the teeth, the woman made her big pitch. The result? She got the lot—the salary she wanted, plus all the fringe benefits she required, including not only a car allowance but free parking, a contribution to her daily gas requirement, and the payment of her tolls to and from Long Island every day.

We are not suggesting that every woman who wants one can appropriate a contribution to a company car dur-ing the course of a closing negotiation. What we are saying is that under circumstances where, for example, the use of a car (or comparable benefit or perquisite) is a virtual precondition to carrying out a job effectively, you should not hesitate to make a firm request for what you feel you need.

Do not accept what you're *offered;* bargain for what you *require.*

Closing is a lonely business. There is no one's judgment to trust but your own. That is what makes it hard—and that is what makes it fulfilling and, retrospectively at least, fun. The culmination of your entire campaign, closing is the point at which the inner driving dynamic of what has been at times a brutal, bone-crushing, spirit-bruising enterprise is finally drawn together and resolved.

Everything jells.

The participants are satisfied.

The best deals always offer something for everyone. Your prospect feels good because he's added talent to what (one hopes) is an already talented organization. You feel good because your efforts have been justified by solid, entirely acceptable results.

Hands are shaken, perhaps an employee contract or letter of employment is signed. You, the cool professional, remain poised and somewhat detached while all this goes on. Somebody says how pleased they are about the outcome of events. You nod and enthusiastically agree. There is the conventional exchange of platitudes about the future, outstanding opportunities, what an asset you are, how challenging it will be to work together on upcoming enterprises. Nods all around. More smiles. Arrangements are made for a starting date.

Then you leave. Tomorrow you will tell your current employer of your future plans. (Nicely, of course—you never know when you may need him.)

Once home, you feel—perhaps uncharacteristically—like having a drink. Nothing beats a good belt, you say to yourself, at a moment like this. Or a long, slow joint. Or even, bless us all, some sex. Perhaps all three. You've spent weeks being controlled, disciplined, and fastidious in most of what you've done, written, and said. Now, briefly, you are entitled to hang loose, to dream about the infinite possibilities of future, even more thrilling, coups. Now, fleetingly, there is only rising applause, several curtain calls, and shouts for the star.

You made it.

12

PAYDIRT

THE MORALITY
OF THE JOB HUNT

In terms of marketing, you've got to have the will to
win. You've got to see the blood running down the
street. You've got to be able to take it. You've got to be
able to shove it. If you're not, you're nobody. You never
will be. You think you are? Fine. Love it. Go on—have
happiness, have love, have this, have everything. But
as far as marketing is concerned (which is what *really*
counts)—*nyenta*. Nothing.

—CHARLES REVSON*

IT'S ALL THERE. From
someone who knew. The
top-job hunt, especially for women, is an assault course. It
can be run successfully only by those prepared to take
punishment, to ride roughshod over a dozen different ob-
stacles, to push relentlessly against intransigence, to work

---

*From Andrew Tobias, *Fire and Ice: The Charles Revson-Revlon Story*
(New York: William Morrow, 1976).

grueling hours in the planning, promotion, and the making of that sale. There are precious few easy stretches. It's a demanding struggle all the way.

Ambition is the most democratic disposition in the world. Provided it is underpinned by carefully considered, realistic objectives, it's unstoppable. Revson had it. As Tobias reports, Revson, nasty, ruthless, brilliant, crude though he was in his life, was, professionally, a man of "single-minded persistence and drive, entirely dedicated to his business." And that's the way you have to be in your job hunt.

But ambition, needless to say, has its darker side. Any business encounter, and especially one with an important job opportunity hanging on its outcome, involves an element of mutual moral ambiguity. The ethics of business can be reduced to a subtle distinction between equivocation and deception. The former has to do with a sophisticated awareness of the self-interested limits, under certain circumstances, of total frankness. The latter has to do with the cynical, premeditated expression of deliberate falsehoods.

The temptation for you to cross that fine line between equivocation and deception increases (unless you are an individual of inordinate personal integrity) in direct proportion to (a) the duration and level of development of your campaign; (b) your lack of confidence about your chances of closing a particular opportunity; and (c) your lack of competence to adequately discharge the responsibilities associated with a job you have set your heart on winning.

Ambition's negative corollary is the tendency to overreach. The more committed you are, the more vulnerable you become to committing an impropriety. Which is, incidentally, another justification for casting a wide campaign net. Because the more opportunities you create for yourself, the less inclined you will be to compromise your standards in pursuit of the so-called main chance.

Our advice is simple. Begin an immediate analysis of the implications your new job will have for your career as a whole. Has the focus shifted in an appreciable way? And if so, how and to what extent? The fact is that the most successful people in modern business life are constantly redefining themselves as individuals and, more particularly, as commodities. New jobs, especially those that are important and powerful, represent two kinds of opportunity. The first has to do with self-fulfillment. The second with the future.

And the future starts now.

That means informing those people with whom you have had discussions during your job hunt about the nature of your new situation. Send a note of thanks and, where appropriate, invite those precious new contacts to approach you at any time if there is anything you can do for *them*. It is a criminal waste of a major career resource not to try to convert at least a portion of those contacts into lasting business associations. Men do it. Women have to learn to do it too. (Interestingly, while we researched this book we found evidence of a powerful "old girls' network" in the New York communications industry. For us, it was a wonderful source of research leads; for them, it remains an invaluable talent bank.) Executed cleverly, a modest keeping-in-touch effort may insulate you from the necessity of ever having to construct so elaborate a job-hunting campaign again.

And there is something else you should consider. Since future opportunities will multiply according to the prominence of the job position you have recently secured, you would be foolish not to revise your résumé in the light of your new responsibilities. An outdated résumé is for "also rans." Redraft it now.

You never know when you may want it.